Philosophy

WHAT EVERY CATHOLIC SHOULD KNOW

Philosophy

WHAT EVERY CATHOLIC SHOULD KNOW

Peter Kreeft

IGNATIUS PRESS
San Francisco

AUGUSTINE INSTITUTE
Greenwood Village, CO

Cover Design: Ben Dybas

Copyright © 2023 Ignatius Press, San Francisco
And the Augustine Institute, Greenwood Village, CO
All rights reserved.
ISBN 978-1-955305-31-0 (pbk)
ISBN 978-1-955305-30-3 (hbk)
ISBN 978-1-955305-32-7 (ebook)
Library of Congress Control Number: 2022949965

Printed in Canada ∞

Contents

Introduction 1

Part I: Epistemology 9

1 What Is Philosophy? 11

2 What Good Is Philosophy? 14

3 What Is the Best Method for Philosophy? 16

4 Where Should Philosophy Begin? 20

5 Is There Objective Truth? 25

6 Must We Just Trust Reason, or Can We Prove
by Reason that Reason Is Trustable? 28

7 Are Philosophical Reason and Religious
Faith Natural Enemies or Allies? 31

8 Is Knowledge of Truth an End in Itself? 33

9 How Does Human Knowing Work? 36

10 How Is Self-Knowledge Possible? 40

11 Is There Any Knowledge that Transcends Reason? 43

12 Is It Possible for Human Reason to Know God? 46

Part II: Metaphysics 49

13 What Is Being? 51

14 Is Being One or Many? 55

15 Are Universals Real? 59

16 Are Essences Real?   64

17 Are Substances Real?   67

18 Are Categories Real?   70

19 Is Spirit Real?   73

20 Is Change Self-Contradictory? How Can the
    Same Thing Become Different?   78

21 Are There Degrees of Reality?   81

22 What Is the Connection between Metaphysics
    and Ethics?   84

Part III: Special Metaphysics: Cosmology   87

23 What Is Man's Relation to Nature?   91

24 Is Causality Real?   94

25 Are There Four (Kinds of) Causes?   97

26 Are Final Causes (Teleology) Real?   99

27 Is Time Real?   103

28 Is Hierarchy Real?   107

29 Is Evolution Real?   111

30 Is Time Travel Possible?   114

31 How Can We Prove the Uniformity of Nature?   118

32 Is the Universe Real Independent of Thought?   121

Part IV: Special Metaphysics: God   125

33 Is God Real?   127

34 What Is God? Who Is God?   131

35 How Can We Know God?   135

36 If There Is a God, Why Is There Evil?   138

37 What Is the Relation between God and Time?   141

38 Can Free Will and Divine Predestination Be
    Reconciled?   144

39 Can God Create Something Out of Nothing?   147

40 Does God Transcend Logic?   150

41 Is the Idea of the Trinity Self-Contradictory?   153

42 Why Is Theism More Rational than Pantheism
    or Deism?   156

Part V: Philosophical Anthropology   159

43 What Is the Soul?   161

44 Which Is Prior, Intellect or Will?   163

45 Do We Have Free Will?   166

46 What Is the Role of Emotion?   169

47 What Is the Meaning and Importance of Sex,
    Marriage, and Family?   173

48 Is Mankind Good or Evil?   176

49 What Motivates Us to Be Wicked?   179

50 What Is Happiness, and How Can We Achieve It?   184

51 Is the Soul Immortal?   187

52 What Happens at Death?   190

Part VI: General Ethics   195

53 Does Ethics Depend on Religion?
    On Metaphysics? On a Philosophy of Man?   197

54 What Are the Most Important
    Moral Virtues?   201

55 Is Morality Objective and Discovered, or
    Subjective and Invented?   204

56 Are There Inherent and Inalienable Rights?   208

57 Is Each Person an Intrinsic End?   212

58 Does the End Justify the Means? (Utilitarianism)   214

59 What Makes a Human Act Morally Good or Evil?   217

60 Does Virtue Make You Happy?   219

61 What Is Conscience?   221

62 Aren't There Exceptions to Every Moral Rule?   224

Part VII: Social and Political Ethics   227

63 Is the State Natural or Artificial (a "Social
    Contract")?   229

64 What Is the Ideal State?   233

65 Should the State Have an Official, Public
    Philosophy of Man and Human Life?   236

66 Should Church and State Be Separated?   239

67 Is Democracy the Intrinsically Best Form
    of Government?   243

68 Is Freedom an Intrinsic Good?   246

69 Why Are There "Conservatives" and "Liberals"?   248

70 How Do We Reconcile Solidarity and Subsidiarity,
    the Common Good and the Individual Good?   251

71 What Is the Purpose of Punishment?   255

72 Is War Ever Just?   258

Appendix: Other Philosophical Questions   263

Concluding Unscientific Postscript   265

Introduction

This is a book about philosophy, not theology, and I have appealed to philosophical reason rather than religious faith for most of my premises. However, philosophy and theology often overlap, since they address some of the same questions. And the theological consequences of a philosophical position (like nominalism, for instance, or materialism) are often revolutionary. These are only some of the many reasons why religious believers should know something about philosophy.

As the title indicates, this book is especially for Catholics. It is written by someone who not only believes all the articles of faith the Church teaches but also sees important philosophical issues involved in these articles of faith.

On the other hand, this book is for many different audiences:

- readers who are Catholics but not philosophers;
- readers who are philosophers but not Catholics;
- readers who are both Catholics and philosophers;
- readers who are neither Catholics nor philosophers but are interested in both; and
- even mere "social climbers" who want a token "Catholic" book on their bookshelves only to impress and deceive their friends and to make themselves look fashionably open-minded and ecumenical as well as somewhat "intellectual."

Nearly everything in this book should be of interest not only to Catholics but also to all other Christians, and not only to Christians but also to other religious believers—and not only to religious believers but also to unbelievers who are interested in philosophical issues simply because they are human beings with human reason. But Catholics have historically been the religious group most ready to embrace philosophy and to reject both mere fideism (faith alone, without reason) and mere rationalism (reason alone, without faith). Our first pope, Saint Peter, commands us to "be ready always to give a reason of the hope that is in you" (1 Pet 3:15, KJV). On the other hand, if we do not begin with faith and hope in reason itself, we will not begin to philosophize, for we will not trust our instrument.

This book is designed for readers on various levels of philosophical knowledge; and the levels of its chapters are not the same: some are more difficult and abstract than others. I saw no need to arbitrarily keep the same level of difficulty in the content of the chapters. In fact, when that is done, the level is almost always closer to Oprah's rather than Aristotle's. The content should determine the form, not vice versa, since the varied subject matter demands some chapters should be longer than others in quantity, and some be more difficult than others in quality. And this variety is good for pedagogical reasons too: students *should* be challenged and even confused about some ideas, and they should find others clear and obvious. So please do not judge the rest of this book by any one chapter.

The close connection between Catholicism and philosophy can be seen not just historically but also logically by a single simple syllogism:

Premise 1: The word philosophy *means "the love of wisdom."* Even though few so-called philosophers nowadays either love or think about either love or wisdom very much, nevertheless that is what philosophy is, by its very essence, and what its three greatest inventors and exemplars—Socrates, Plato, and Aristotle—all explicitly defined it to be. That is an empirical, historical fact, and not a controversial philosophical opinion or a divinely revealed dogma.

Premise 2: Jesus Christ is wisdom itself, divine wisdom, the very mind of God, the Logos, the "light that enlightens every man" (Jn 1:9)—"every man," not just Catholics or other Christians. That is *not* an empirical, historical fact, but it is a divinely revealed dogma that is absolutely central and essential to the Christian faith. Christ is "catholic" with a small *c* (that is, "universal"), as well as "Catholic" with a capital *C* (that is, he is the very visible, particular, and concrete founder of the very visible, particular, and concrete entity that identifies itself as the "one, holy, catholic, and apostolic Church").

Conclusion: It logically follows from these two premises that there is more than just a "connection" between the essence of Christianity (which is Christ himself) and the essence of philosophy (which is the love of wisdom).

It should not be surprising, then, that many of the greatest philosophers of the last two thousand years have been Christians, for example, Justin Martyr, Augustine, Boethius, Dionysius, Erigena, Anselm, Abelard, Aquinas, Bonaventure, Scotus, Ockham, Eckhart, Cusa, Machiavelli, Descartes, Pascal, Leibniz, Locke, Berkeley, Kant, Kierkegaard, Newman, Marcel, Teilhard de Chardin, von Hildebrand, Chesterton, Maritain, Gilson, and MacIntyre.

In the Introduction to his encyclical on faith and reason, *Fides et Ratio*, Pope Saint John Paul II said (religious) faith and (philosophical) reason are like the two wings of the one bird that is our soul, by which the bird flies. That has always been the centrist "mainline" position exemplified by Catholic philosophers. It is distinct from fideism, rationalism, and dualism, all of which see these two things as opposed or at least in a problematic relationship rather than seeing them as meant for each other and for fruitful union, like Adam and Eve.

The need for this book is perennial, but it is especially acute today, when both faith and reason are on life support in our culture, which is increasingly hostile to both, or at least to the classical or traditional forms of both. We live in a culture in which traditional versions of both faith and reason, and of both Catholicism and philosophy, are "in crisis," as fashionable writers say, or in "deep doo-doo," as a recent president with a sense of humor put it.

Western civilization used to be called "Christendom," but it has increasingly become first neutral, then secular, then apostate and Christophobic. Most philosophers now identify as atheists; many American citizens identify as not religious, or "nones." And America is the *most* religious nation in Western civilization outside of Poland and Hungary. Our fashionable intellectuals ("the chattering classes") are skeptical of all "metanarratives" or "worldviews," and of "logocentrism," or faith in any "reason" broader than computer calculation, or "analytics."

In this culture it is essential that Catholics and other Christians know the intellectual weapons and strategies of the enemies of religious faith and the defensive and offensive intellectual weapons that defeat them. Philosophical arguments are needed. They are weapons in the intellectual dimension of spiritual warfare, a warfare that is just as real and just as much a matter of life or death as physical warfare. We are informed by our highest authority that "we are not contending against flesh and flood, but against the principalities, against the powers" (Eph 6:12). That is a divinely revealed truth, whether or not it is politically correct to say it today.

Many influential modern philosophers (Hobbes, Voltaire, Hume, Nietzsche, Russell, and Sartre, just to name six) explicitly declare that their philosophies are designed for this spiritual warfare. For instance, the whole second half of Hobbes' classic, *Leviathan*, is an attack on the Catholic Church, which he called "the kingdom of darkness." Voltaire defined the Church as "the infamy" and demanded it be "crushed." Nietzsche even labeled himself "the antichrist," and Christianity as the unique synthesis of all evils.

The *philosophical* battlefield in this war dates from the very beginning of philosophy, with Socrates versus the Sophists. And today's battlefield continues to host the same battles and many of the same essential arguments, pitting Socrates' children against the children of the Sophists. The strongest of Socrates' intellectual children today seem to be the Thomists, and the most influential of the Sophists' children is Nietzsche and his admirers, especially the deconstructionists.

Not to know or care about the identity, strategy, and weapons of the enemy when one lives on a battlefield is as irresponsible as sauntering through a meadow full of land mines, or swinging a butterfly net when bullets buzz through the air.

This book is organized by controversial ideas in each of the divisions of philosophy rather than by chronology. Even though tracing the *story*, or history, of "the great conversation" from Socrates to the present is, to most people, more dramatic and more interesting than tracing the ideas themselves logically through the different divisions of philosophy, yet this book is not organized historically. For it is impossible in one volume to do more than pick a few quick and tiny appetizers out of the rich history of philosophy. (I tried to do that in *four* volumes, in *Socrates' Children*, which, like this book, is designed for intelligent and curious beginners.)

Most of the issues in modern philosophy are critiques or forgettings of common sense, which is found most fully in the philosophy of Aristotle and Aquinas, the two great philosophers who are most missing from philosophers' conversation throughout the history of modern philosophy and right into the present. But this book is not a nostalgic tour of old, forgotten ideas; it is a challenge to mortal combat in a very present "war of the worlds." For words are a world, and so is wisdom.

The issues are perennial. Philosophy has always asked four great questions:

1. What (and how) can I know? (epistemology, the philosophy of knowing)
2. What is real? (metaphysics, the philosophy of being)
3. What am I? (anthropology, the philosophy of self, or human nature)
4. What should I do? (ethics, the philosophy of what is good, both individually and socially)

Logically, metaphysics comes first, for knowing (epistemology) means knowing some *being*, knowing *what is*, and that's what metaphysics is about. Anthropology, which is about what the *knower* is, is also relative to metaphysics, which is about what *is*. For instance, if only matter is, then there is no soul or mind in me as distinct from body or brain. And ethics is also dependent on metaphysics, because what *goods* I should choose, live according to, or strive for also depends on what is real or true (metaphysics). For instance, if moral values are not objectively *real*, then morality is subjective, man-made, relative, and changeable.

But most modern thinkers begin with epistemology rather than metaphysics, for two main reasons: (1) because many are skeptical of the very possibility of metaphysics, and also (2) because the modern mind is no longer the mind of a child, who, forgetting himself, asks, What's that? but the mind of a teenager, who is agonizingly self-conscious and critical, and asks, What am I?

Both sides, the premoderns, who begin with metaphysics, and the moderns, who begin with epistemology, have a point, since being and knowing (the subjects of metaphysics and epistemology, respectively) mutually presuppose each other: being is contained in knowing, and knowing is contained in being. For on the one hand, all knowing is a knowing of some *being* and thus relative to being; but on the other hand, all the being we know is also *known*, and thus contained in our knowing.

One may enter the house of philosophy by either door. We may begin with either epistemology or metaphysics. I have decided to begin with epistemology, even though it is not the easiest, or the most interesting, or the most concrete, or the most important and practical division of philosophy (ethics is all of that); but because that is where most modern philosophers have begun, ever since Descartes, and I am writing to modern readers, not medieval readers (unless they are watching from heaven).

In each of these four divisions of philosophy, I have selected the questions that I see as the most important and controversial today, especially for Catholics, whose traditional "perennial philosophy," like a great old castle, has been increasingly undermined in its philosophical foundations ever since the castle was most completely built, with Aquinas. Almost all the popes since the Counter-Reformation have pointed to Saint Thomas as the most complete and adequate touchstone of philosophical wisdom, though not by any means the only one.

Aquinas' philosophy on nearly every point is compatible not only with the faith but also with common sense, from which modern philosophers have increasingly run away, down a splendidly multifarious confusion of exit roads. That Thomism is simply "common sense" is the main thesis of G. K. Chesterton's *Saint Thomas Aquinas: "The Dumb Ox,"* a book about which the greatest modern scholar of Saint Thomas, Etienne Gilson, has said, "I consider it as being, without possible

comparison, the best book ever written on Saint Thomas."
Comparing Chesterton to other Thomist scholars, he wrote
that "the so-called 'wit' of Chesterton has put their scholarship to shame."[1]

I am honored to be a link in the chain between you and
Gilson, Chesterton, Aquinas, and Truth, which I also capi-
talize since, as a Christian, I believe Truth is a divine Person,
since he said so himself (Jn 14:6).

The content of this book is classical rather than contemporary. It does not mention the controversies that typify most
currently fashionable books of philosophy because they are
usually boring, abstract, technical, undramatic, faddish, and
ephemeral.

---

1   Cyril Clemens, *Chesterton as Seen by His Contemporaries* (Webster Groves, MO: International
Mark Twain Society, 1939), pp. 150–51.

Part I

Epistemology

Epistemology is that division of philosophy that asks questions about human knowing (*epistēmē* in Greek): whether it "works" to know objective reality; *how* it works; and how it *ought* to work, its best method.

Traditional premodern philosophy usually began with and centered on metaphysics, since metaphysics is about being, or reality, and knowing is one kind of being. Every knower is a being, and everything known is a being. But it is also true that every knowing of every being is also a knowing. Thus, epistemology and metaphysics imply each other. This has been called "the gnoseo-ontological circle" or the epistemological and metaphysical circle.

Modern philosophers, beginning with Descartes, usually do epistemology first, because they want to be sure their tools of knowing are adequate to the job before using them to build the edifice of the rest of philosophy. So I follow the modern order and begin with epistemology, even though I think the dependence of epistemology on metaphysics is more basic.

The first few questions are about philosophy itself. This can be classified under epistemology because philosophy is a certain kind of knowledge, or wisdom.

1

What Is Philosophy?

Here are nine answers from the history of philosophy and our present culture to the question of what philosophy is. If you are attracted to answer no. 1, you will probably like this book. If not, probably not.

1. Philosophy is the love of wisdom. This is what Socrates both taught and practiced. Without love, there is no real philosophy. In fact, all four of the Greek words for *love* are involved in philosophy:

- *eros*, or desire (thus philosophy begins not with the proud claim to possess wisdom but with the humble confession to lack it, for we *desire* only what we *lack*);
- *storge*, or instinctive, habitual familiarity;
- *philia*, or genuine, loyal friendship; and
- *agape*, or the charity that gives itself to the beloved.

And "the beloved" in philosophy is not just *knowledge* but *wisdom*, which includes the knowledge of good and evil, a knowledge of values, a knowledge applied to life, a knowledge that makes a difference to your life.

2. Philosophy is an authoritarian (rather than authoritative) pontificating and bloviating, claiming to be wise but not giving good reasons. This is a perennial temptation for parents and teachers of kids who ask troublesome questions.

3. Philosophy is winning arguments by cleverness rather than wise and profound reasoning. This is what made the

Sophists rich in ancient Athens and what makes politicians famous in contemporary America.

4. Philosophy is ideology, a man-made system of ideas and values imposed not by reason but by will and by force if necessary. It is usually political. This is both the Fascist (Right) and the Marxist (Left) concept of philosophy. It is also that of both the establishmentarian pessimist Hobbes (man is wicked; society saves him) and the antiestablishmentarian Romantic idealist Rousseau (man is innocent; society corrupts him).

5. Philosophy is the defense of our prejudices, the ego's rationalization for what the id (the animal self) desires. This is the Freudian claim about all truth claims, and therefore also about Freud's.

6. Philosophy is an expression of "the will to power" over other minds (Nietzsche), the will to dominate other classes, races, or genders (deconstructionism). Philosophy is lighting the fuses of the little dynamite sticks planted in others' brains (Maoists).

7. Philosophy is the activity of refuting other philosophers by analyzing their language and exposing their confusions; it is doing for other philosophers what pooper-scoopers do for dogs. It is, in other words, sorting through the anal product of horned cattle. This is the noble claim of the early "analytic philosophers."

8. Philosophy is the profession of professors who inhabit a "philosophy department" in a university. It is a game played to get tenure by sophisticated scholarship that perhaps five or six other persons in the world care about. It is not about life; it is a tiny department in life, confined to an increasingly small number of offices and classrooms on an increasingly large university campus.

9. Philosophy is whatever you want it to be, since, as our parents and pop psychologists often assure us, "you can be whatever you want to be." In other words, you are God.

You are omnipotent. In fact, you are more omnipotent than God, since God cannot change his very being, but you can change yours. So you trump God. Perhaps you will become president.

2

What Good Is Philosophy?

The question regarding what good is philosophy assumes that the correct answer to what philosophy is, is "the love of wisdom."

What good is philosophy? What can you do with it? These are the questions philosophy students are always asked, especially by their parents. The parental assumption is that the philosophical question philosophy majors are destined to ask most frequently after they graduate is, Do you want fries with that?

The answer to the question about what you can do with philosophy is nothing. But it can do something with you if you surrender to it. That's also the only good answer to the question, What can you do with marriage? A philosophy, like a spouse, is not a product but a love.

Old Aristotle, and most of his ancient and medieval followers, answered our second question by saying there are three possible motives for seeking truth: improving the material world around you (technology and the arts), improving your behavior (morality, both individual and social), or improving your very self, your mind (philosophy, and also pure science as distinct from practical, applied science).

It seemed obvious to Aristotle and most premoderns that the three motives are in a hierarchy of interiority and importance. Our civilization has reversed that hierarchy. But this book is not an apologetic for a dodo bird. Philosophy is dying, but it is not yet dead. In fact, as Gilson has said, "Philosophy always buries its undertakers."[1] Reading this book is an exercise in responsible conservation. Isn't philosophy more worth conserving than the box turtle, the piping plover, or the snail darter?

Philosophy alone cannot save your soul, but it can help. If philosophy is the sincere love of wisdom, and if Christ is supreme wisdom, divine wisdom incarnate, then philosophizing is, in itself, by its own essence, the (usually unconscious) search for Christ.

If Christ does not lie, then "he who seeks finds" (Mt 7:8) is also true of all true philosophers, if not in this world, then in the next. For Christ clearly did not mean "he who seeks finds" to apply to the seekers of money, sex, and power by greed, lust, and pride, but to the lovers of what his Father was: truth, goodness, and beauty; wisdom (which is deeper than knowledge); sanctity (which is deeper than propriety); and joy (which is deeper than happiness, as happiness is deeper than pleasure). We can fail to attain these things, but we cannot fail to want them, for the human heart was designed in heaven, not in Hollywood or Harvard.

"He who seeks finds" does not mean all philosophers will go to heaven. Some philosophers, when they die and meet God, and God gives them the choice between going to heaven or going to a philosophical lecture on heaven, would choose the lecture.

---

1 Etienne Gilson, *The Unity of Philosophical Experience* (San Francisco: Ignatius Press, 1999), p. 246.

3

What Is the Best Method for Philosophy?

Methods, unlike truth, are pragmatic and relative. There are methods that are better or worse, but there is no one absolutely best method for the love of wisdom.

A method is a "means" to an end. And, of course, "the end justifies the means." That's what a "means" *means*. The principle that "the end does not justify the means" means only that an end, however good, does not justify a means that is intrinsically evil. Feeding the poor is a good end, but cannibalizing the rich is a bad means to it.

The end of philosophy is wisdom. Following are some of its most useful methods that have been invented and used by philosophers:

- The Socratic method of interpersonal dialogue by logical questioning, especially about the essence or "what" of an important concept. This method is used in Plato's dialogues, which are the very best introduction to philosophy, in my experience.
- The Aristotelian method of observation of the whole of ordinary experience, especially (but not exclusively) sense experience, and abstracting universal essences from diverse and changing accidents. (This is also essentially the method of what is called phenomenology.)
- The medieval Scholastic method of a debate between contrary authorities according to the demands of formal

logic, especially syllogisms, as used by Aquinas, especially in his *Summa Theologica*.

- The pragmatic method of tracing the practical consequences of any ideas that make a difference to your life. This method was used by Pascal, William James, and some "existentialists."
- The Hegelian method of looking for instances of the dialectical pattern of (1) thesis, (2) antithesis, and (3) apparently paradoxical synthesis. This method was used not only by Hegel but also by his opponents such as Kierkegaard and Marx.
- The Cartesian scientific method of (1) beginning with universal methodic doubt, (2) dividing problems into parts and taking them one by one, (3) ordering your steps from simple to complex, and (4) reviewing all your work for possible errors or omissions.

None of these methods is exclusive and definitive, but all are useful.

Following are some of the methods that are the most constricting and deforming to philosophy:

- The rationalist method of demanding that all ideas be absolutely clear and distinct, and that every conclusion be deduced with absolute certainty.
- The empiricist method of Hume and the early analytic philosophers such as Ayer and the early Wittgenstein, which reduces all meaningful judgments to sense observations or logical tautologies.
- The Kantian "transcendental" method of doubting our ability to know objective reality or "things in themselves" and seeking the subjective rather than objective conditions of possibility for the knowledge we all have.

- The ideological method of judging all ideas by their "political correctness." Machiavelli, Marx, Hobbes, Rousseau, Dewey, Mao, and Mussolini all teach this method, with very different political results.
- Consulting one's own most passionate feelings as the touchstone and supreme authority. This method is used by "spoiled brat" teenagers, "touchy-feely types," and potheads.

Most of the recommended methods are roads that by their nature lead to religious faith if used honestly, as in fact has often happened in the history of philosophy, or that lead believers into deeper dimensions of their faith, as also has often happened.

If you interpret our third question about method as meaning, "What method do you recommend I use as a beginner in choosing what important classics to read in philosophy?" I reply that you cannot do better than to trace philosophy's own history, which is like a long conversation.

Therefore, begin with Plato's early dialogues (*Apology*, *Ion*, *Meno*, *Gorgias*, *Phaedo*, and *Republic*) and proceed to Aristotle's *Nicomachean Ethics* and then either Epictetus' *Enchiridion* or Marcus Aurelius' *Meditations*. Add Lucretius' *On the Nature of Things* for a charming ancient Roman classic of anti-religious materialism.

Then move to Augustine's *Confessions* (Sheed translation, please!), Boethius' *The Consolation of Philosophy* (Green translation), Anselm's *Proslogion*, and an edited version of Aquinas' *Summa Theologica* (like this author's *A Summa of the Summa*) for the best of medieval thought.

Shift to Descartes' *Discourse on Method*, Pascal's *Pensées*, Kant's *Fundamental Principles of the Metaphysic of Morals*, Bretall's *A Kierkegaard Anthology*, and Marcel's *The Philosophy of Existentialism* for some of the most important of the "good guys" in modern times.

And read Machiavelli's *The Prince*, Hume's *An Enquiry concerning Human Understanding*, Ayer's *Language, Truth, and Logic*, Marx's *Communist Manifesto*, and Sartre's *Existentialism Is a Humanism* for the modern "bad guys." Each of these modern classics is mercifully short.

4

Where Should Philosophy Begin?

Philosophers sometimes speak of the "Archimedean point," after the Greek scientist Archimedes, who discovered the power of the lever and wrote, "If you give me a lever long enough and a fulcrum to rest it on, I can move the whole world." One's starting point determines everything else.

Believers are naturally tempted to begin with the most certain beginning, which is God, who "can neither deceive nor be deceived."[1] But we are not God (call the reporters!), and we *can* be deceived about anything, including God. It's true, as the medievals taught, that divine authority is the most certain of all arguments; but it's also true, as they also taught, that human authority is the weakest of all arguments. It's true God invented and created human reason, but how can reason itself prove that? If we use God to justify reason and reason to justify God, we are arguing in a circle. On the other hand, if we use reason to prove itself we are also arguing in a circle. (See chapter 6 for a way out of this problem.)

We have here a dilemma: if we begin with faith in God, we are not doing philosophy, for we are not appealing to reason but to faith. That is not philosophy but theology, and that is fine when teaching other believers, but it is not effective when addressing unbelievers or doubters. On the other

1   *Catechism of the Catholic Church* (*CCC*), no. 156, quoting Vatican I, Dogmatic Constitution on the Catholic Faith *Dei Filius* (April 24, 1870), ch. 3.

hand, if we begin with ourselves and our human reason and experience, we are resting our philosophy on a very fallible platform. Ed Muskie, a Democratic presidential candidate back in the 1970s, gave a speech to Republican farmers in Iowa after climbing onto a manure spreader since there was no other platform high enough, saying, "This is the first time I have given a Democratic speech from a Republican platform." Ronald Reagan told this same story in one of his speeches with the parties reversed.

I think there is no way out of the dilemma except to accept our own fallibility honestly and humbly, and therefore that of all our philosophies. All the sciences except mathematics have succeeded by beginning there, with that confession of fallibility. Descartes' starting point of methodic doubt is scientific and useful, but his demand for philosophy to supply the kind of certainty only mathematics gives simply cannot be met.

But some humanly fallible starting points are much weaker than others. Ideology, passion, personal preference, and comfortable prejudices are the weakest starting points. Common sense, common experience, and common logical principles are the strongest.

This starting point is especially strong when the two blades of human reason's scissors, the logic of the intellect and the experience of the senses, are combined, as in Aristotle. Modern philosophy's first great debate was between epistemological rationalism (e.g., Descartes) and empiricism (e.g., Hume); between demanding the claims of sensation be judged by reason and demanding the claims of reason be judged by sensation. That question is answered only by combining rather than opposing these two powers, the mind and the senses, as Aristotle did. (See chapter 9 for Aristotle's explanation of how knowledge best works. Aristotle is conspicuously absent from the minds of most modern philosophers.)

Two things are necessary for this combination to work: first, that experience not be narrowed to purely external sensory experience, or "sense data," as in the physical sciences; and second, that the mind not be narrowed to a calculating computer.

This last point needs a more detailed explanation. The logic of the intellect, as distinct from that of a computer, consists essentially of three "acts of the mind" and the three mental powers behind them: (1) the power of understanding the meaning of concepts (like "man" and "mortal"), (2) the power of knowing truth by making judgments about concepts (like "all men are mortal"), and (3) the power of deducing some judgments (conclusions) from others (premises), like "all men are mortal, and I am a man, therefore I am mortal." A computer cannot begin where we begin: it can judge and calculate but not understand.

Most of our mistakes in judgment are based on mistakes in understanding—that is, on "mis-understandings." That is why Socrates spent most of his time in his dialogues carefully defining terms, as a good painter spends most of his time on the surface preparation. Aquinas answered nearly all his opponents by pointing out their confusion between two meanings of a key term, one of them accounting for the error in their position and the other accounting for its partial truth. We are usually deceived by half-truths, not by sheer and total falsehoods.

That is one of the reasons for preferring the old, commonsensical, ordinary-language logic of Aristotle, which begins with the first act of the mind—understanding—rather than modern mathematical logic, or "propositional calculus," which is preferred by analytic philosophers and begins with the second act of the mind—propositions judged as simply true or false, like a digital computer.

The following is a stretch, and not typical of the clearer and simpler points in this book.

It is a fairly technical point that you will probably understand adequately only later.

The philosophical controversy behind the two logics (ancient Aristotelian ordinary-language logic and modern symbolic logic, or digital logic) concerns whether or not we can know real universal essences or natures (such as "man" and "mortal"). Most premodern philosophers affirmed we could. The technical term for this position is "epistemological and metaphysical realism." Most modern philosophers assume we cannot; universal essences are not realities but only names. The technical term for this position is nominalism (literally, "name-ism").

If there are no essences, there are no essential distinctions; and if there are no essential distinctions, there is no essential distinction between essences and accidents, and between essential distinctions (such as the distinction between a man and an animal) and accidental distinctions (such as the distinction between a Black man and a White man). Thus, a nominalist cannot logically justify antiracism because if there is no such thing as a single universal essence or essential nature of man, then one cannot distinguish that (nonexisting) essence from accidents like race, gender, or other features that are nonessential. If there is no one universal human essence, then if we will, we can classify Blacks and Whites, or Jews and Gentiles, as groups that are as different and incomparable as men and animals, because according to nominalism all classifications and categories ("universals") are merely names we subjectively invent and impose on reality rather than objectively real kinds, natures, or essences God or nature has made. Modern nominalists, like deconstructionists, attack this notion of natural kinds or classes or essences, and judgments based on them (such as "all men are created equal") as logocentrism, the assumption that Logos, or universal meaning, is objectively real and discovered rather than invented and imposed by our will.

And, of course, no orthodox Christian can be a nominalist because the two most central and distinctive dogmas of Christianity are the Trinity and the Incarnation, and both of these use and presuppose the distinction between universal natures or essences and individual persons, since the doctrine of the Trinity affirms that three divine Persons have the same essential divine nature, and the doctrine of the Incarnation affirms that the one divine Person of Christ has two natures, human and divine. Nominalism also contradicts the Catholic dogma of transubstantiation, for if there are no essences, there cannot be a distinction between the accidents or appearances of bread and wine, which in the Eucharist do not change, and the essence, which does change from bread and wine to Christ's Body and Blood.

In light of Saint John the Evangelist's identification of the Logos with Christ (Jn 1:1–14), antilogocentrism, and the nominalism that is its basis, must be identified as not a Christian philosophy or even a neutral one but an anti-Christian philosophy.

5

Is There Objective Truth?

People say very silly things about truth nowadays, for instance, "That's your truth, not my truth," which is saying we each live in a different world, a different universe, or a different dream. If that is literally believed, it is a good definition of insanity. Fortunately, people don't always mean what they say. That's why some Christian philosophers say they are nominalists.

What people mean by asking if there is objective truth is really five different things, five different questions:

1. Is the essential meaning of the concept "truth" the conformity of our subjective thoughts to objective reality? Or is it something else, such as logical consistency, practical workability, coherence among ideas—anything that helps us integrate our experience—or political correctness?
2. If truth is this conformity to reality, is truth discovered by our mind or by something else?
3. If truth is objective (the answer to question 1) and discovered by the mind (the answer to question 2), can we discover it by ordinary experience and thinking or by the scientific method or by both?
4. If we can discover it by both, including ordinary experience, is there also objective truth about universally binding moral values as well as material facts?

5. If the answer to that question is yes, is there also objective truth in religion? (For religion includes but also goes beyond moral laws. Every religion also makes truth *claims*.)

One can deny objective truth in sense 5 alone (religious), or in both 5 and 4 (moral), or in 5, 4, and 3 (ordinary), or in 5, 4, 3, and 2 (mental), or in all five senses.

One can also make the distinction between two questions, the first one metaphysical and the second epistemological. The metaphysical question is, Does objective truth *exist*? The epistemological question is, Can we *know* it? One could answer yes to the first question and no to the second, as some skeptics do. Perhaps truth is the top of Mount Everest, but we are only ants.

Skepticism is the denial of our ability to know truth. The problem with skepticism is that all expressions of it seem self-contradicting. For instance,

Is it true there is no truth?

Is it possible to know the truth that it is impossible to know the truth?

Is it an objective truth that truth is not objective?

Is it only probable and never certain that all truth is only probable and never certain?

Is it only subjective that truth is only subjective?

Is it universally true that no truth is universal? If "all rules have exceptions," that one does too.

Is it unchangeably true that no truth is unchangeable?

Is it an absolute truth that there is no absolute truth?

We should also distinguish five different questions that are often confused:

1. Does X exist?
2. If so, can we know it exists?
3. If so, can that knowledge be certain?
4. If so, can we prove that certainty to others?
5. If so, can we do it by the scientific method?

Obviously, many things exist (question 1) that we do not know (question 2), such as whether extraterrestrial life exists or whether there is beer in heaven.

And most of our knowledge (question 2) is only probable (question 3), such as that a meteorite will not fall out of the sky, land on my head, and kill me tomorrow, or that the next time I click on the "help" icon I will not suddenly actually receive the help I needed. (I think each of those two events has actually happened only once in the history of the world.)

And some of our certainties (question 3) are private and cannot be proved to others (question 4), such as the certainty that I am self-conscious or feeling pain. I might be a robot or a Stoic.

And even many philosophical conclusions that have been proved with certainty by sound deductive arguments (question 4), such as the arguments of Socrates to prove justice is a virtue or of Aquinas to prove an uncaused cause exists, do not use the scientific method (question 5). There is no way to prove by the scientific method that all valid proofs must be by the scientific method. Scientism (scientific reductionism) is self-contradictory.

6

Must We Just Trust Reason, or Can We Prove by Reason that Reason Is Trustable?

If we are about to build a house or a bridge or a rocket ship, we should first be sure our tools are up to the job. Rusty saws, vague measuring instruments, or dirty fuel will doom our endeavors. But how can we examine our *mental* instrument, which is our reason, the instrument doing the examining?

It must be either by something less than itself, something more than itself, or itself.

It cannot be justified by something less than itself, something like animal instinct, passionate desire, our sheer willfulness, or financial success. The higher authorizes the lower, not vice versa. Reason may justify trusting something subrational, but something subrational cannot justify trusting our reason.

Human reason can be justified by something more than itself, by God as its Creator and Designer. But how do we know there is a God except by using our reason? Even the act of faith presupposes the use of reason, for example, to distinguish the God we believe in (who is perfect) from the gods we do not believe in (which are imperfect). You have to know how to read before you can read the Bible. Even if reason can prove God's existence, you can't use God to prove reason and also use reason to prove God without arguing in a circle.

But human reason cannot prove itself either. Imagine twenty prisoners on trial. One of them leaps up into the judge's seat and declares all twenty prisoners innocent, including himself. The twenty prisoners are all our acts of reasoning; the judge is that act of reasoning that declares all twenty innocent.

To make the last point by another analogy, the part cannot justify the whole, so the *part* of reason that is to justify reason as a whole cannot justify reason as a *whole*. It is involved, not detached.

It is immanent, not transcendent.

So the only possible answer to the question is that it is an impossible and unfair question, an unjust demand. We simply *must*, and we *do*, assume reason, trust reason, as soon as we begin to think. In that sense, faith (faith in reason, not necessarily faith in God) must precede reason. In fact it always does.

Modern philosophy begins with Descartes' demand to solve this so-called "critical problem" of the justification of reason. All three major schools of classical modern epistemology accept the question (which I think is their common mistake) and then give three different answers: reason justifies both itself and sensation (rationalism, e.g., Descartes); it is sense experience that tests, justifies, and limits reason (empiricism, e.g., Hume); and Kant's critical idealism, which contends reason creates its own Logos, its own truths and forms and categories and meanings, like a creative artist, rather than discovering them, like a humble scientist. (Kant called this his "Copernican revolution in philosophy.")

All three epistemologies fail to answer the question. Rationalism fails because of the analogy of the prisoners on trial. Empiricism fails because it logically leads to skepticism, as Hume showed. And Kantian critical idealism fails because it contradicts itself in asserting we can know, as an objective truth or a "thing in itself," that we do not know things in themselves but only the appearances we ourselves subconsciously create or form.

What is Aristotle's answer to the question? It is very simple: he never raises the question. He accepts his tools (reason and the senses) and uses them. And they work. The proof of the pudding is in the eating. That's usually called common sense. The two modern philosophers who come closest to this, Reid and Moore, both defend common sense as the necessary beginning and source of philosophizing. But they are the exceptions rather than the rule in modern philosophy.

Perhaps our inability to answer that question is not as important as modern philosophers think, if philosophy is the love of wisdom, and if wisdom is needed by everyone, not just by philosophers, and if wisdom is for life, not just for thought. If you were promised the wisest possible answer to any question at all, which question would be at the top of your list? Would it be how reason can validate or justify itself? Or would it be how we can find truth, goodness, beauty, and joy?

7

Are Philosophical Reason and Religious Faith Natural Enemies or Allies?

When we speak of reason and faith, we can mean either the human *acts* of reasoning and believing or the *objects* of those acts, the truths known by reason and the truths known by faith.

The relation between faith and reason *as human acts*—in other words, the relation *in our souls* between our rationally proving and our religiously believing—is complex, mysterious, and somewhat different for different people. But the relation between *the truths known* by human reason on the one hand and *the truths known* by religious faith by Christians (and, for the most part, Jews and Muslims too), by believing their religions as divine revelation, is simple and clear and universal.

(I mean by "knowing" or "reasoning" here all three acts of the mind: understanding, discovering, and proving.)

Obviously, according to unbelievers, faith and reason are enemies, and according to believers, they are allies—or at least not enemies. For if reason can prove faith to be false and unbelief to be true, then faith and reason are enemies, because the true and the false are enemies.

Believers argue they are allies for two reasons: (1) because both the truths known by reason and the truths known by faith are sets of *truths*, and only falsehood, not truth, can contradict truth; and also (2) because the same God is the source of both reason and faith. He is the source of both the design and creation of the human reason and intelligence, and he is also the source of the religion that is the revelation of truths about himself. In other words, truth does not contradict itself, and God does not contradict himself.

But what of "the war between science and religion" that is the main theme of modern intellectual history? For half a millennium, we see science continually growing and religion continually declining. Surely, the relation between these two developments is not mere coincidence.

The answer to the psychological, subjective question is complex, for human motives are complex. But the answer to the rational, logical, objective question is simple. The war is a myth. It does not exist. It has not produced a single casualty. There is not a single essential religious truth claim that has ever been refuted by a single discovery by a single scientist or science. There have been many misunderstandings and many polemical *attitudes* on both sides, but attitudes are not arguments.

So the next time you hear people talk about a war between those two abstractions, "science" and "religion," turn the discussion from safe abstractions to concrete particulars: ask them which discovery of which science, proved how and when and by whom, has contradicted and refuted which doctrine of which religion. You may make your opponent surprised at his own surprise at his silence.

8

Is Knowledge of Truth an End in Itself?

If anyone has the right to be called the repository of the pre-modern mind, it is Aristotle, whom the medievals called "the master of those who know" (Dante) and simply "*The* Philosopher" (Saint Thomas Aquinas). Aristotle is also the philosopher most conspicuously absent from most modern philosophers' writings, unless as an object of misunderstanding, personal allergy, and ire, as in Bacon and Hobbes. And if anyone has the right to be called the founder of the modern mind, it is Francis Bacon, the main mind behind the modern scientific method. So let us set these two philosophers against each other.

Aristotle answers the question in our title yes, and Bacon answers no.

Bacon's argument for his no is that the whole premodern world, Greek as well as Christian, was naïve and childlike in being contemplative rather than active—that is, in prizing knowledge simply for its truth rather than its power. Bacon announces the most radical revolution possible, a new "summum bonum"—"greatest good," "final end," or "meaning of life"; and it is "man's conquest of nature" by applied science rather than God's conquest of man by truth, goodness, and beauty. It is the conquest of suffering by the transformation of this world into a heaven on earth by technology, which is the real point or payoff or value or "bottom line" of science. C. S. Lewis puts this tectonic shift in philosophy into two sentences in *The Abolition of Man* when he writes: "For the wise men of old the cardinal problem had been how to conform the soul to reality, and the solution had been knowledge, self-discipline, and virtue. For magic and applied science alike the problem is how to subdue reality to the wishes of men: the solution is a technique [i.e., technology]."[1]

What is Aristotle's argument for the superiority of the contemplation of truth over technology's active "conquest of nature" and of the natural ills "that flesh is heir to" (Shakespeare, *Hamlet*, 3.1)? It is very simple and commonsensical. He divides the motives for seeking knowledge into three, and thus he divides the sciences that result from them into three kinds. The technological sciences Bacon puts first, Aristotle puts last because their end is only improving and having power over *our material world* outside of us. Higher in importance are what Aristotle called the "practical sciences," or sciences of practice, especially ethics and politics, because they perfect *our actions*, our lives. They are higher in importance because they are closer to home: they perfect our own lives rather than the external things we own and use. But highest of all in importance are the "contemplative" or "speculative" sciences, which seek truth for its own sake (both truth about things below us in nature and truth about supernatural things above us), because they perfect not our world or our acts but *our very selves*, in perfecting a distinctively human power of our souls, namely, our mind and understanding.

Financial statistics about the disproportion between university money invested in the STEM courses and money invested in the humanities and the arts show how much our world has moved from Aristotle to Bacon. Whether this movement is a progress or a regress depends on our values. There was a philosopher long ago who was clearly on Aristotle's side when he uttered my candidate for the most practical

---

1   C. S. Lewis, *The Abolition of Man* (New York: HarperCollins, 2001), p. 77.

sentence about profit and loss ever spoken: "What does it profit a man, to gain the whole world and forfeit his life?" (Mk 8:36; cf. Lk 9:25). By that man's standards, Saint Thomas Aquinas, who "baptized Aristotle," picked his philosophical friends wisely.

The apotheosis of man's conquest of nature, argues Lewis in *The Abolition of Man*, is the conquest of *human* nature: the deliberate redesigning and control of our own nature. The conquest of nature is not complete until nature's trump card, death, is conquered, probably by genetic engineering. If you want a preview of a world of immortals, just leave a dozen eggs out on your kitchen table for a year, then smell. As Lewis says in *Mere Christianity*, "We are like eggs at present. And you cannot go on indefinitely being just an ordinary, decent egg. We must be hatched or go bad."[2]

If the *power* over nature that technology gives us is not conformed to the moral *goodness* that ethics gives us, and if ethics is not conformed to *truth* about ourselves and the meaning of human life, we will not evolve into something superior but devolve into something inferior, something like moral infants with adult weapons. If we have evolved from apes in our bodies and our brains, we can also "go ape" and devolve back into apes in our souls and our spirits.

---

2   C. S. Lewis, *Mere Christianity* (New York: HarperCollins, 2001), p. 199.

9

How Does Human Knowing Work?

There are four fundamentally different answers to the basic question of how human knowing works: Aristotelian realism, Cartesian rationalism, Humean empiricism, and Kantian idealism.

The best way to understand the three modern epistemologies is by beginning with Aristotle's and then seeing how each one differs from that. This is the best way to understand them for two reasons: first, because that is how "the great conversation" that is the history of philosophy actually unfolded, each system reacting to, and providing what they thought was a better alternative to, the previous system; and second, because Aristotle's system corresponds the most to common sense, and it is much easier to understand departures from common sense by beginning with common sense than to do the opposite.

For Aristotle, it is an evident fact all our knowledge begins with and depends on experience, especially sensory experience. Those born blind have no "innate ideas" of colors, and no immediate intuitive access to what Plato called the "forms" or "ideas," the essential natures of things. (Plato, like Descartes, was a rationalist.) We have the *power* or potentiality of reason innately, by nature, but not any actual, factual content knowledge innately. So Aristotle is an empiricist. Experience is our first teacher.

But he is a "soft empiricist" rather than a "hard empiricist" because he holds that although our knowledge begins with experience, it does not end there. For reason can take our knowledge to a second level by abstracting universal and unchangeable essences from many particular instances that change and differ in their accidental properties. For instance, we can understand what is universal in human nature from our experience of many different human beings, abstracting this essence from accidents like gender, race, and age. This "inductive abstraction" is not only an abstraction of the universal from the particular but also of the essence from the accidents, and it is a power that most modern philosophers doubt, downplay, or deny.

This "abstraction" involves not only a movement from many concrete particulars (e.g., men) to the single abstract universal class that contains them (e.g., mankind), which a computer can also do, but also, simultaneously, an *understanding* of the essence or nature of the universal that is thus abstracted, which a computer cannot do. For if we did not understand *what* to abstract, we could not abstract it; and if we did not abstract it, we could not get it into our minds.

Only after we get these universals can we deduce conclusions from them. The universals are our premises. A valid deduction always requires at least one universal premise.

Thus, there are four steps, each of which depends on the one before it. For instance, first we observe people dying. Then we inductively arrive at the universal truth that "people die." Then we understand this dying is necessary and essential to us (because the body is part of our essential nature). Only then can we validly deduce that we, too, will certainly die.

The difference between Plato and Aristotle as regards our starting point in epistemology can be seen by the following analogy. Plato says we are born with universal ideas or forms in our minds; that is like saying lions are born in zoos. Aristotle says we have to go outside of our minds into the jungle where lions actually live and "abstract" them from the jungle and bring them home to our inner zoo (our minds) and put them in cages (mental concepts).

Descartes, the father of modern rationalism, sees this traditional Aristotelian and Thomistic epistemology as naïve and uncritical. He wants to begin with universal doubt rather than a practical faith in both reason and the senses; and the only way out of this universal doubt is to find a truth that cannot be doubted because it is self-evident and its denial is self-contradictory. That is not to be found in sense experience but in reason alone, so Descartes' rationalism begins with reason, not sensation, and then deduces everything from that, since deduction alone, unlike induction, yields certain conclusions. ("Induction" here refers to the nondeductive kind of reasoning, the third act of the mind, not intuitive "inductive abstraction," which is the first act of the mind and which begins with the sense experience from which we abstract universal essences.)

Descartes' empiricist critics like Locke deny we have "innate ideas" and, like Aristotle, hold that in fact all our knowledge depends on sense observation. But without the power of abstraction, we cannot move from this sensory beginning to any certain knowledge beyond sense experience, which is always changeable and uncertain; and Hume drew from this premise the natural conclusion of skepticism. He says it is only our subjective habit, not any objective reason, that moves us to think we know essences, substances, universals, or principles, including even the principle of causality that is essential to all the sciences.

Kant, like Hume, found rationalism uncritical but he also found Hume unlivable. A merely Humean being is not a full human being. Kant sought to join reason and sensation, which both rationalists and empiricists had separated; but he did so by saying reason, rather than abstracting universal forms from particular material instances, imposed its innate universal categories onto the material of experience like a projection machine in a theater projecting the images in its film onto a movie screen. This is true, Kant said, (1) of the sensory categories of time and space, (2) of logical categories like cause and effect, substance and accident, and (3) of the three basic metaphysical ideas of self, world, and God.

So for Kant, what we know is not what is, not "things in themselves," but only the work of our own minds. We are artists who create order in the world rather than scientists who discover it. This is not subjective in the sense of arbitrary and individual, but it is necessary and universal. We all experience the world in basically the same way because all minds have the same structure and powers. In other words, our common world is like a common dream.

It is man, rather than God, that says "Let there be X" and there is X. If Cartesian rationalism is too proud and uncritical, and Humean "hard empiricism" too humble, Kantian idealism seems to combine both errors. Its ideas are as innate as rationalism's, and its skepticism of knowing objective reality is even greater than Hume's.

So it's back to Aristotle then, and common sense. Sometimes, when you're on the wrong road, going back is the only way to go forward.

10

How Is Self-Knowledge Possible?

"Know thyself" was the commandment written over the entrance to the temple of the oracle at Delphi, and Socrates took it as his life's task. But how?

Animals apparently have surprisingly sophisticated kinds of consciousness of the world, but no self-consciousness. They have social shame but not individual guilt. They have no "identity crises." It is not knowledge but self-knowledge that distinguishes us most clearly from mere animals.

We know self-knowledge, or self-consciousness, is possible because we know it is actual. But there is a problem in accounting for it. It is a problem because the essential meaning of "knowing" is a relationship between two opposite poles of the act of knowing, the knower and the known, the subject of knowing and the object of knowing; and it seems they cannot be identical because the subject stands behind the glass, so to speak (the window or the telescope), and the object stands in front of it. The very same person, it seems, can't at the same time stand both behind and in front of, or both inside and outside. To use another analogy, knowing is like an arrow: it points in one direction, outward. The arrow points to something beyond itself, something other than itself. But self-consciousness, or self-knowledge, means the knower is pointing to himself, not to anything other than himself.

Self-knowledge seems to become even more impossible when I realize that even if I were to know every single fact about myself, I could not, at that same time and in that same act of knowing, know every single fact about myself because my act of knowing all those facts is creating a new fact about myself.

To use a physical analogy, knowing is like light: it takes time, so the physical object that I *know* by vision at this moment is really not the physical object that *exists* at this moment; it is the object as it was a split second ago. With regard to distant objects like the sun, this time gap is considerable: about eight minutes. If the sun exploded now, we would not see it or feel it until eight minutes later. The time gap in self-knowledge is between the first act of knowing, the act of knowing all the *past* truths about the self, and the second, *new* act of knowing, by which the first act itself is now included in the object known by the second.

This problem is like the problem of how we know other minds: philosophers don't have a good, clear answer to it. But it's not a real, "existential" problem because we all know we do have self-knowledge, at least imperfectly. My point in mentioning these problems is not that they are important, but that they are not! Yet philosophers love to speculate about them.

Another such speculative problem is the "brain in a vat" problem: How can you be certain you are not really a brain in a vat in a mad scientist's laboratory, only dreaming the world you see every day because the scientist is feeding it into your brain? How do you know the so-called real world is not merely the Matrix? How do you know the devil is not hypnotizing you? If these problems are real problems for you, I gently suggest you go to a psychiatrist rather than a philosopher. And I ask forgiveness from ordinary, more practical readers for taking them along on a shaggy-dog story.

An existentially real and consequential thought experiment, on the other hand, is Robert Nozick's happiness machine. Suppose you could enter a machine that would give you perfect, unrelieved happiness without cost, without boredom, and without end. It gave you everything you ever wanted except truth. Would you enter the machine? In his *Pragmatism*, philosopher-psychologist William James suggests there is a great gap between two kinds of people, the "tender-minded," whose absolute is ideals like happiness and goodness, and the "tough-minded," whose absolute is facts and objective truth. Everyone wants truth, and everyone wants happiness, but which comes first if they conflict? If your answer is there is no one right answer for everyone, you are probably tender-minded. If your answer is there is, you are probably tough-minded.

Do you believe (or disbelieve) in God because it makes you happy and good or because it is true? Do you think God prefers an honest unbeliever or a dishonest believer? If you say the first, you probably believe honesty would eventually lead to belief; if you say the second, you probably believe belief would eventually lead to honesty. Even though both of these beliefs are true, the question remains.

I suspect we are all tough-minded deep down, because when we were three and believed in a real Santa Claus, we were very happy (and very good!) every December 24; but we cannot simply return to that belief because we know it is not true. For the same reason, I think we know, or deeply suspect, that God admires an honest, truth-seeking unbeliever more than a dishonest, truth-ignoring believer. Choices are important, especially choices about God; but motives are even more important because they reveal what you are, not just what you do.

I hope we are all tough-mindedly honest deep down, but I wonder, especially when I read *Brave New World* and watch it become more a depiction of reality with every generation.

11

Is There Any Knowledge that Transcends Reason?

If there is any knowledge that transcends reason depends on what you mean by *reason*. Let's begin by defining *reason* in the broad, ancient sense of the "three acts of the mind": (1) understanding the meaning of a concept, (2) knowing truth by a judgment, and (3) proving some truths (conclusions) by reasoning from other truths (premises).

A true but too-easy answer to the question is that since we are far from omniscient, *everything* transcends our reason in some respects. Saint Thomas said no man has ever known everything there is to know about anything, even about a flea. All three kinds of knowledge in us are imperfect. Regarding the first act of the mind, there is a great difference between the way in which we can understand the concept of the number three, for instance—with total or almost total understanding and clarity—and the way we can understand the concept of God—with radically inadequate understanding and clarity. Regarding the second act of the mind, there is a great difference between the certainty of the judgment that 11+3 does not equal 2 abstractly and the realization that that judgment becomes false on the face of a clock. And there is a difference between the certainty of both of these judgments and the certainty of the judgment that God will choose to forgive all my sins. And regarding the third act of the mind, there is a great difference between the clearly valid argument that "All men are mortal, and I am a man; therefore I am mortal" and the validity of Einstein's equations in his proofs of the theory of relativity, and even of some of Euclid's demonstrations in his geometry.

Beauty, music, humor, prayer, and mystical experience are five examples of things philosophers have never clearly, definitively, and adequately understood, and which seem to transcend reason in a way in which other truths do not, even controversial ones like "God exists," "virtue makes us happy in the end," and "an inefficient democracy is better than an efficient dictatorship."

Theories about all five of these phenomena almost always seem to concentrate on one aspect of it. For instance, beauty is harmony, music is waves, humor is irony, prayer is conversation, or mystical experience is blotting out self-consciousness.

All five give us not just pleasure, and not just happiness or satisfaction or contentment, but joy.

Music is "the universal language." Perhaps it is the language God used to create the world, and the language we spoke in Eden before Babel. It seems not only to evoke feeling but to possess meaning, but a meaning that always transcends translation into words.

Beauty is what first impresses us about truth and goodness. It is their child and their ambassador. It is the quality of all objects of love, as Plato taught in *The Symposium*. And it gives us an ecstasy, a "standing outside yourself," a blissful loss of self-consciousness; yet it is recognized only by persons, who have self-consciousness, not by animals, which do not.

Humor is part of the image of God in us, the God who invented gooney birds, ostriches, penguins, platypuses, blobfish, and the even stranger creatures that appear in our mirrors. It helps us survive our incessant waves of overserious hate, war, and despair. But it is not merely rational. Rationally explaining a joke destroys it!

Prayer, too, like lovers' mutual gazes, transcends its clumsy words. It is essentially the practice of the presence of the Indefinable One.

Mystical experience somehow seems to transcend and negate the fundamental law of conscious reason, the dualism between knower and known, subject and object. It is apparently negative in many ways (it is *not* rational or ordinary or clear or natural, etc.), yet these negations both reveal and conceal something that is really infinitely positive. All ways of attempting to express rationally whatever it is that it puts in the place of ordinary consciousness fail.

I deliberately left these descriptions short, ragged, and unprofessional. All five of these things come to us not in words but in waves. They are like forty-foot waves, and we have no surfboards to ride them. The syllable that expresses them best is *O*; the syllable that expresses them worst is *I*.

12

Is It Possible for Human Reason to Know God?

How can the finite know the Infinite? How can the fallible know the Infallible? How can we fools know divine Wisdom?

The answer must avoid the two opposite alternatives of dogmatism and skepticism. Our knowledge of God is radically inadequate yet real. We can never comprehend him, yet we can apprehend him. We cannot know him as we know our inferiors or our equals, but we can know him somewhat as our cats and dogs know us. Rationalism is out of place here but so is irrationalism. Religion would not exist if we did not have *some* knowledge of God, something that is not just willing or feeling.

It is a radically inadequate knowledge, but even that old pagan deist Aristotle knew that "the slenderest knowledge that may be obtained of the highest things is more desirable than the most certain knowledge obtained of lesser things."[1] By "the highest things" Aristotle meant the gods, which for him were many, though they were all subordinate to the one uncaused cause. They were distant and impersonal; yet even this radically defective theology moved him to make that profound value judgment of his, which even most Christians today seem to doubt.

---

1 Saint Thomas Aquinas, *Summa Theologica* I, q. 1, a. 5 ad. 1, referencing Aristotle, *De Partibus Animalium*, bk. 1, ch. 5.

We have to choose between what Saint Augustine called "perfect knowledge of imperfect things" (i.e., creatures) and "imperfect knowledge of perfect things" (the things of the Creator). Medieval man prioritized that first thing, namely, imperfect knowledge of perfect things (God and the things of God), which is theology; modern man prioritizes the second thing, more perfect—certain, clear, adequate—knowledge of imperfect things (the things of this world), which is science and technology. That is probably because medieval man, like a child, was more concerned with objective reality, with the quality of the objects known, than with himself, with the quality of the knowledge, while modern man is the opposite.

What kind of knowledge is this radically imperfect "knowledge" of God that we have? Saint Thomas says it can be only of two kinds. We have no clear, literal, and univocal positive knowledge of what God is, of God's essence or nature. Our clear and literal knowledge is only of what God is *not* (God is not an equation or a star or an animal). Our knowledge of what God *is*, is all analogical rather than univocal. It is not a knowledge of what God is but of what God is *like*, or rather of what is like God. If we want positive knowledge of God, we must be satisfied with analogical knowledge. God is more *like* a good shepherd than a bad one, and more *like* a shepherd than a sheep, but he is neither, literally.

This makes philosophical theology still possible but humble. It avoids the dilemma of proud and presumptuous rationalism versus despairing and skeptical irrationalism. The analogy of our pets is useful here: our cats know what we are not, but they do not know what we are. They know we are not cats or cat food, but they cannot know our essence, our reason, or our conscience.

The issue is somewhat parallel to the dilemma of pantheism versus deism. Pantheism makes God too close in making God everything and therefore making everything God, including ourselves. Deism makes God too far away in denying any relationship with God, and therefore reducing religion to the-istic philosophy.

Think of God as Mount Everest. Rationalists see themselves as helicopters capable of flight to the summit. Irrationalists think of themselves as rocks incapable of even the first move-ment upward. We should think of ourselves as rabbits, capable of only a few hops in the right direction. But even that little bit counts, for a rabbit who hopped ten feet up is twice as far from the ground as one who hopped only five feet up, though both would be very, very far from the top. But the thought of us rabbits hopping to the top of Mount Everest is absurd.

The living God will not sit still on a chair in our photog-raphy studio and let us snap his picture. But we *need* to know God, the true God, more than we need to know anything else. The divine solution to that dilemma is revelation.

This fits the hierarchy of beings. The higher the being, the more active it is, the more it reveals itself. Numbers do noth-ing; they are ideas, not entities. Stones are entities but don't live or grow. Plants live and grow but don't have desires or movement. Animals have desires and movement but can't rea-son. And within the species of rational animals there is more hierarchy. Babies can't speak, and children need to listen to parents, and students need to listen to teachers. If we are to know the true God, we need to listen to him, and the activity must come first from his side; he must come down the moun-tain to us, since we cannot climb up to him.

And that is exactly the claim of the three Abrahamic reli-gions. Religion is the relationship between God speaking and our listening and believing. Religious faith, which argues, "God said it, I believe it, that settles it," may sound like irra-tionalism; but it is not. It is a very reasonable thing in almost all the dimensions of life except conflicts like war, politics, and competitive sports. It is called trust. If we can't trust God, whom can we trust? Ourselves?

Part II

Metaphysics

Metaphysics means literally "beyond physics." This does *not* mean metaphysics is the division of philosophy that deals only with nonphysical things or spiritual things or the supernatural. It means metaphysics goes "beyond" physics in *scope*, or universality: it deals with *all* beings, and all kinds of being, not just some. It deals with being itself—being as such, "being qua being."

The fundamental division between two kinds of being is the distinction between being itself and beings, that is, between *being* as one, infinite, and eternal and *beings* as many, finite, and temporal. Thus, we have three subdivisions of metaphysics: (1) general metaphysics, about being in general or all being; (2) the special metaphysics of the finite and temporal being, or the cosmos, which is cosmology or philosophy of nature; and (3) the special metaphysics of infinite and eternal being, or God (this is also called philosophical theology or natural theology or rational theology).

General metaphysics centers on three questions:

1. What does it *mean* to be real? What is being? (This will be the question in chapter 13, and the most abstract and difficult one.)
2. *What* is real? What kinds of things have being? (These are the more specific and concrete questions in chapters 15–21. They presuppose the answer to, What is being?)

49

3. What is the relationship between metaphysics and the rest of philosophy, especially ethics? (That is the question for chapter 22, and the most practical.)

13

What Is Being?

In a real sense, what being is, is the most difficult of all questions. For in asking whether something has being, or has existence, or *is*, we are always presupposing we know what *is* means, what it means to *be*. And in one sense we clearly do know, for we all know how to use the word *is* or *be* or *being*. And yet in another sense we do *not* know, for when we are asked to define it, or even just to explain it, we find we can't. We define other things in terms of being (e.g., "Man *is* the being who has animal life and rational thought"; or "God *is*, but Santa Claus is not"; or "To *be* or not to be, that *is* the question"), but we cannot define *being* in terms that are any more basic.

Nearly all premodern philosophers affirmed the possibility and priority of metaphysics; but the majority of typically modern philosophers deny it, usually because their epistemologies are too restrictive. For instance, Hume's empiricism limits knowledge to the empirical, and Kant's critical idealism limits knowledge to phenomena, or appearances to us, not things-in-themselves.

The problem with both of these restrictive epistemologies is they are self-contradictory. Empiricism is self-contradictory because the self that knows empirical objects is not itself an empirical object; and Kant's denial that we can know things-in-themselves, or objective truth, is put forth as the objective truth, a thing-in-itself.

Another reason many modern philosophers give for believing that metaphysics is simply impossible is that it has no specialized, definable, circumscribable subject matter. No newspaper headline ever revealed new facts about it. No one ever said, "Hey, have you heard about what being did yesterday?" Yet, though metaphysics does not have a distinctive and definable subject matter, it does have a distinctive and definable point of view. It seeks the truths or properties or principles or laws that are common to everything, to all things, to all real beings.

We have a natural and innate curiosity about all being, about everything. We resist all walls to our knowledge and insist on knowing what is on the other side of the wall. And that is not just blind stubbornness, but it is reasonable. For as Ludwig Wittgenstein said, "To draw a limit to thinking we should have to be able to think both sides of this limit."[1] Take a minute to think that through. There is no way out of it. Thus, all skeptical or restrictive epistemologies are self-contradictory. And that includes ones that eliminate metaphysics.

There is also a good *positive* reason for thinking our innate and universal desire to do metaphysics, to know all that has being, corresponds to a reality that can satisfy that desire. For all other innate and universal desires correspond to realities that can satisfy them. If there is a hunger, there is a food that corresponds to it and satisfies it: truth for curiosity, sexual pleasure for sexual desire, friendship for loneliness, beauty for the desire to see beauty, drink for thirst, rest for weariness, balm for pain, interest for boredom. Thus, objective reality and the subjective desire of the mind to know the nature of reality must correspond, somehow. Subjective mind and objective reality, thought and being, are correlative to each other, made for each other, like men and women. As Jacques

1   Ludwig Wittgenstein, *Tractatus Logico-Philosophicus*, trans. C. K. Ogden (London: Routledge & Kegan Paul, 1922), 27, quoted in John Gibson and Wolfgang Huemer, eds., *The Literary Wittgenstein* (New York: Routledge, 2004), p. 58.

Maritain says, "There is a nuptial relationship between mind and being." That is the hidden but real presupposition of all philosophy, all science, and even common sense.

We implicitly raise the metaphysical question—the question of "to be or not to be," the question, Why is there something rather than nothing?—in many common human experiences. For instance, (1) when death threatens to remove our own being or that of one we love; or (2) when we are surprised by the reality of a specific grace or gift, especially that of the existence of the person we deeply love; or (3) when we feel a cosmic gratitude for all things, because nothing apparently *has* to be, yet everything that is, *is*; or (4) when we are in despair over everything and just wish it would all disappear; or (5) when we are in total boredom and no longer care whether anything is or is not.

We swim in being, as in a shoreless ocean. We cannot avoid being. We can only avoid asking questions about it. But we can also avoid that avoiding; we can be philosophers.

There are many possible answers to the questions, What is being? What is it to be?

Whatever answer is given by any philosopher to the question of what being is will inevitably influence everything else in his philosophy—what man is or what the cosmos is or what God is.

Metaphysical idealism says that being is indistinguishable from idea or consciousness; that being is a subdivision of thought or consciousness or spirit or mind. That was the position of the Greek pre-Socratic philosopher Parmenides and of the modern German philosopher Hegel and of Hindu mystics like Shankara. They say even matter is only thought, or a form of thought, or "inside" thought. At the opposite extreme, materialists like Democritus and Lucretius among the ancients and Hobbes and Marx among the moderns say that to be is to be material. They say even thought is only matter. So a lazy immaterialist would say "it doesn't matter," and a lazy materialist would say "never mind."

Pluralists say many things have being, but there is no *one* being, only many beings and many kinds of being. At the opposite extreme, monists say only unity, and not plurality, is real. And since unity does not change and since in order for things to change, there must be a plurality of states (before versus after), monists do not believe anything really changes. (How, then, do they expect pluralists to change their minds and become monists?)

Platonists believe true being is essence, or essences: the Platonic ideas or forms.

Aristotelians believe primary beings are substances.

Thomists believe being is, most perfectly and actually and ultimately, the act of existence rather than essence.

Atheistic existentialists believe being in the first place is simply human existence.

Taoists and Heideggerians believe being is potentiality rather than actuality.

Nietzsche believes "the will to power" is "the innermost essence of being."

Nihilists believe being is nothingness.

Punsters believe being is what bees do.

Sometimes, the profoundest answer is the silliest-sounding one.

And sometimes it's not.

14

Is Being One or Many?

An American and an Englishman were arguing about whether the word *neither* is pronounced "nee-ther" or "nigh-ther." The Scotsman solved the dispute: "It's nay-ther."

And the obvious answer, the Scotch answer, the common-sensical answer, to whether being is one or many is that it's "nayther" monism (no manyness) nor pluralism (no oneness).

Monism and pluralism are both not only untrue to common sense and experience but also logically self-contradictory.

Monism is self-contradictory because it entails the denial of differences, so that must include the difference between the *correct* answer to the question of the "problem of the one and the many," which, according to monism, is monism, and the *incorrect* answer, which, according to monism, is pluralism.

The commonest form of monism is pantheism, in which the one and only being is divine and perfect. Instead of being the Creator of all things, the God of pantheism *is* all things. Parmenides, a pagan Greek; Shankara, a Hindu mystic; Spinoza, an excommunicated Jew; and Hegel, a heretical German Christian, were all pantheists. According to pantheism, everything is God; therefore, these four thinkers were all God. But even if none of them was really different from God, as pantheism claims, yet they were really different from each other. Parmenides was really not a Hindu, and Shankara was not a Jew, and Spinoza was not a German, and Hegel was not a Greek. So therefore God, who is Parmenides, is not God, who is Shankara. And "God is not God" is self-contradictory.

Pluralism, if it means the denial of real oneness, is also self-contradictory because the meaning of "many" presupposes a one "something" that there are many of. Pluralism entails the denial of any one field in which any twoness, including the twoness of monism and pluralism, fight it out. If monism and pluralism have nothing at all in common, they cannot be different. (What they have in common is they are both "isms.") This applies to all pluralities. For example, men and women are different genders only because they both share gender; and humans (rational animals) and beasts (nonrational animals) are different only because they are both animals; and two and three are different only because they are both numbers. Nothing (except perhaps the essence of twoness itself) can be just two; every two must be two *somethings*, two of some one common something.

Everywhere in the real world we find a manyness organized into a oneness and a oneness organized into a manyness. We find this in galaxies, in architecture, in music, in biological organisms, in a book, in human history, in government, and in a story, just to take eight examples of different kinds of beings. One cannot even imagine or conceive of any of those eight real things as a one that does not include many, nor as a many that are not parts or aspects of a one.

Everything that is, is one. Even a group is one group.

Everything finite is also many. For "finite" means "this and not that." Everything finite has a border, a limit; and whatever is inside that limit is different from whatever is outside that limit. Only if there is a single unique Being that is infinite can there be a "one" that is not also many—unless that one unique Infinite Being is also many—that is, not one of many beings "outside" it but a one Being that is also many "inside" it, which is the case according to Christianity, where the one and only God is a Trinity of Persons. The Trinity is the ultimate reconciliation of the one and the many.

But *in what way* is all being one, and in what way is it many? What *makes* being one, and what makes being many? What *accounts for* the fact that real things are many, and what accounts for the fact that all things are in some way one?

The most obvious answer is they are one in that they all *are*—they exist—but they are many and different in *what* they are. All things that exist have existence in common, and what distinguishes them is their nature or essence, their *what*.

Essence here is used not as distinct from *accident* or *accidental property* but as distinct from *existence*. Essence as distinct from existence means all of *what* a thing is, including both its essential properties and its accidental properties. All things are one in that they all are, or exist; and they are many in *what* they are. Planets and plants, thoughts and things, angels and atoms, all exist, but they have different essences.

So essence is the principle (i.e., source) of differences, of limits, of finitude; while existence is the principle (i.e., source) of oneness, and is in itself unlimited, but limited only by essence, from "without," so to speak, as a river is limited by its banks.

Are you a bit confused by these very abstract concepts? Did you think you got that point clear? Wait till you hear what comes next.

We just said the principle of differences or manyness is essence and the principle of oneness is existence. Yet it is also true that the principle of manyness is existence and the principle of oneness is essence. For two beings may have the same essence (e.g., two human beings) but different acts of existence; that's why they are two, not one. If one dies, the other can still live. So it is existence that individuates while essence universalizes. Each thing has its own act of existence but shares its essence with other things. Essences are "universals," like humanness, or circularity, or blueness, or justice.

So, essence both differentiates and unifies, and existence both unifies and differentiates.

Whenever you bump up against a paradox like this—that is, two points that are obviously both true but seem to contradict each other—you come to an important fork in the road. You have to choose between (1) doing what overly rationalistic philosophers tend to do, namely, resolving the paradox by denying one of the two apparently mutually contradictory facts of experience that produced the paradox or (2) accepting both facts of experience and trying to reconcile them by more carefully defining and distinguishing the meanings of your terms. This is what Augustine did with the paradox of predestination and free will and what modern physicists did with the paradox of light being both a continuous wave and discontinuous particles. And even if the attempt of reconciliation is not successful, you still don't deny the data. You affirm both halves of it. That's what every good story does in showing us both predestination and free choice. Every story, whether real or fictional, must have both predestination on the part of the author and free choice on the part of the characters, even though it does not explain how this is possible. Even if we do not know *how* it is possible, we know it *is* possible because it is actual.

The best way to do metaphysics is the second way: to let the concrete and commonsensical facts of experience judge the abstract theory rather than questioning the data of experience because of the theory. That's what is done in good science as distinct from bad science: the data judge the hypothesis rather than vice versa.

That general principle is more universal and more important than the particular case of essence and existence. So let's just be satisfied with that lesson alone for now. It's enough for a start.

15

Are Universals Real?

Very few people deny that red roses, dark days, just acts, human beings, and triangular pyramids exist. But what about redness itself, darkness itself, justice itself, humanness itself (or "human nature"), and triangularity itself? Do the things designated by those adjectives exist as well as the things designated by the nouns they modify? If not, why can we make true statements about them? If so, where are they?

They are called "universals" because each is both one and many, one quality or property or essence or nature or "something" that is somehow related to or found in many things. Redness is one, but red things are many. Human nature is one, but human beings are many. We live in a universe, not merely in a uni or in a versa. As we saw in our last chapter, it is both one and many. It is obvious where we find the many particulars (e.g., red things), but where do we find the one (e.g., redness)? I can give you red things in your hand, but I can't give you redness.

The history of philosophy has produced four different answers to the problem of universals.

Plato says they exist in objective reality in themselves, apart from and independent of the individuals they characterize. Even if all red things in the universe ceased to exist, redness would still exist. This position is often labeled extreme realism, or extreme metaphysical realism—"realism" because it says universals are real and "extreme" because it says they are real independently of particular things.

Aristotle brought Plato's forms down to earth and made them the forms of substances, of concrete individual things. He says they exist in objective reality but only in the things they modify as their forms (their natures, their "whatness"), either accidental forms or essential forms. If all red things in the universe ceased to exist, redness would not still exist anywhere in objective reality, according to Aristotle. This position is often labeled "modified (or moderate) metaphysical realism"—it is "realism" because it says universals are real, and it is "modified" or "moderate" because it says they are not real in themselves but only in things. Our mind abstracts them from the concrete things in which they exist.

A third position is a bit tricky. It is called conceptualism, and it exists in two versions. Peter Abelard (twelfth century) says universals are only concepts, not realities, but they are based on reality, on real *likenesses* or similarities between individual things. Kant (nineteenth century) agrees they are only concepts but says they are *imposed* on reality, subconsciously but necessarily and universally, by all minds. This is Kantian idealism. Kant says we cannot know they exist in objective reality; we can know they exist only in thought. But some of them, at least, are clear and right thoughts, and some are necessary and unavoidable, such as time, space, cause, effect, substance, accident, self, person, duty, God, and world.

A fourth position is nominalism, and begins with William of Ockham (fourteenth century), who says universals exist only in confused thought, thought that forgets the differences that exist between all things. They are neither realities nor clear concepts but only confused concepts and names (*nomini*) we use as a kind of shorthand, as common names that make proper names unnecessary. Instead of giving a proper and unique name to each red thing or to each rose, as we do to each other, we use a vague, general name like *red* or *rose*. Ockham went so far as to call a universal a "flatus vocis," which is

Latin for "a fart of the voice." Since this position reduces universals to only names, it is called nominalism, or "name-ism."

The issue sounds supremely abstract and impractical. But in fact, it is one of the most practically important issues in philosophy, and it makes an enormous difference which answer you give to the question of whether universals are real. It may not make an important difference when it comes to roses or redness, but it makes a great difference when it comes to human beings and human nature. If there is no such thing in objective reality as human nature, then we cannot have any such thing as an ethics of "natural law." We cannot ground ethics in human nature and its needs if human nature is not a reality. Nor can we distinguish the natural from the unnatural. We cannot say that any human act is wrong because it is unnatural or harmful to human nature, such as sodomy or polygamy or transgenderism or suicide or genocide or cannibalism. We can only say (1) it is rare in fact, or (2) we do not personally like it, or (3) we have agreed by will and convention to discourage it by somehow penalizing it.

Also, if we are consistent nominalists, we cannot say all humans are equal in their essential nature if there *is* no such thing as any real universal essential nature; and then we are open to racism and "inferiorly human" subspecies if we wish. Only our own will and choice restrains us, not our mind recognizing reality. In other words, our will and power replace truth.

Also, if we are nominalists, we must end in skepticism, because deductive arguments, which are the only ones that yield certainty, must have at least one universal premise in order to be logically valid.

On the other hand, if we are Platonic extreme realists, then human nature is more real than individual human beings; abstract things are more real than concrete things. This can be dangerous, especially to political idealists who ignore real human individuals for the sake of "humanity."

As usual, Aristotle's is the middle position of common sense that avoids opposite extremes. Aristotle affirmed Plato's universals, but not as independently existing realities, like gods, but as real properties or attributes of things.

Augustine added to Aristotle by giving Plato's ideas their other home, as ideas in the mind of God the Creator and Designing Artist.

Aquinas combined Aristotle with Augustine by saying universals exist in three places: (1) "before things" in the mind of God as the Designer, as Augustine said; and (2) "in things"— that is, in objectively real, concrete particular material things, as Aristotle said, as their forms; and also (3) "after things" as concepts in the human minds that have abstracted them from those things, as the conceptualists said. (But Kant said we do not abstract them but impose them.)

From the commonsensical Aristotelian point of view, which of the two errors and extremes about universals, Platonism or nominalism, is the more dangerous? The history of philosophy gives us a clear answer to that question. The Platonist quite naturally modifies his Platonism and becomes an Aristotelian and/or an Augustinian; but the nominalist either converts out of his nominalism or moves toward Hume's skepticism or Nietzsche's nihilism. (For Nietzsche, there is no being; being itself is "a vapor and a fallacy" because it is a universal.)

When we first discover the obvious distinction between universal principles and particular instances of them, or between universal laws (either the laws of nature or the laws of morality) and diverse applications of these laws to diverse situations, we are thrilled to find a home for both of our instinctively believed truths: there are indeed universal and unchangeable principles *and* there are special cases and circumstances that need more than the knowledge of principles; there is need for both principles and creative applications of them.

When we first discover there is a home for both universals and particulars, we discover the alternative to both the dogmatism that ignores the changing, contingent, and unpredictable particulars and the skepticism that ignores the unchanging, necessary universals. The same light dispels opposite darknesses: both dogmatic, legalistic, mechanistic rigidity and unprincipled, random, willful relativism.

16

Are Essences Real?

An essence is an answer to the question, *What* is it? What is its essential nature?

This is not exactly the same as the question, Are universals real?; but it is closely related to it, because all essences are universals, although not all universals are essential—some are accidental. For example, rationality is essential to man, but maleness is not; life is essential to roses, but redness is not. So the question about essences, which seems very abstract and theoretical, is whether there is a real distinction between the essential (or the substantial) and the accidental. We are here asking not about the distinction between essence and existence but about the distinction between essence and accident. (Essential forms and accidental forms are both examples of essence in the broader sense—essence as distinct from existence, *what* it is as distinct from *whether* it is. And this distinction between the essential and the accidental is itself an essential distinction, not an accidental one, if we are not to absolutize the relative or relativize the absolute.)

If there is no such thing as the human essence, or essential nature, then we can exalt what common sense sees as an accident, such as race, to the position of an essence, and we can then say that either Blacks or Whites are not really fully human because they lack that accident, now misperceived as essence. Or we can do the same with gender and say men and women do not share the same human essence but are two different species: "men are from Mars, women are from Venus."

And if there are no common essences, we can say about every individual what Aquinas says about angels: they are so individualized that each one is a different species;[1] they differ not as Fido and Rover differ but as dog and cat differ. And that is almost what our culture now says about individuals in their total autonomy and identity. It has moved from John Donne's "No man is an island" to Simon and Garfunkel's "I am a rock, I am an island."

And if we can make an accident into an essence, we can also make an essence into an accident. We can also reduce an essential difference such as rationality to something accidental and thus erase the essential difference between man and beasts. And we can do this either by treating animals as persons and ascribing to them human rights, or by treating humans as animals and enslaving them, killing them, or eating them at will—all of which, of course, have often been done in human history and none of which can validly be condemned if there is really no essential difference between the essential and the accidental, which is the case if this distinction is merely our choice, our desire, our invention, or our prejudice. We can say we don't *like* this prejudice, but we can't *justify* rejecting it. The will or the feelings replace reason. The morality of relativism and subjectivism is the natural consequence of the metaphysics of nominalism.

And if there are no essences, then there is no teleology, "final causality," or natural ends; nothing, including human beings, can have essential purposes, ends, destinies, or goods if there are no essences. In that case all ends are relative and subjective, chosen by will or felt by emotion, and imposed on a world that is in objective fact nothing but blind, purposeless matter.

---

1   Saint Thomas Aquinas, *Summa Theologica* I, q. 50, a. 4.

This theoretical philosophy of being leads to a practical philosophy of life that we find in Ecclesiastes ("Vanity of vanities! All is vanity," Eccles 1:2) and *Macbeth*:

> To-morrow, and to-morrow, and to-morrow,
> Creeps in this petty pace from day to day
> To the last syllable of recorded time,
> And all our yesterdays have lighted fools
> The way to dusty death. Out, out, brief candle!
> Life's but a walking shadow, a poor player,
> That struts and frets his hour upon the stage,
> And then is heard no more; it is a tale
> Told by an idiot, full of sound and fury,
> Signifying nothing.[2]

What is the meaning of life? Nothing. Whatever you want it to be. This "existential" nihilism is a logical consequence of metaphysical nominalism. And it is the deeper, hidden cause of the decline of Western civilization. The most abstract philosophical issues have the most concrete practical consequences.

---

2   William Shakespeare, *Macbeth*, ed. Joseph Pearce, Ignatius Critical Editions (San Francisco: Ignatius Press, 2010), pp. 115–16.

17

Are Substances Real?

The term *substance* in philosophy does not mean the same thing as *substance* in chemistry—that is, an element on the atomic table or a compound of elements, an arrangement of atoms that makes for a specific kind of matter. In philosophy, a substance is simply a noun, a thing, an entity, a being that exists in itself rather than in another thing as one of its properties. For instance, a man is a substance but his actions, passions, place, time, possessions, causes, effects, qualities, quantities, and relations to others, though they are real, are not substances but accidents.

And an accident, in Aristotelian terminology, does not mean an event that happens on a highway when the brakes fail or in the back seat of a car when a condom leaks. Grammatically, philosophical accidents are usually expressed by verbs, adverbs, adjectives, prepositions, or conjunctions, while substances are expressed by nouns.

Modern empiricists like Hume deduced, from the empiricist premise that we can know only what we perceive, that substances were not real, since we never perceive a substance, only accidents. We perceive the color, shape, and size of a rock, but we do not perceive that which possesses all these accidents. We do not see or hear or feel rockiness.

So if we are both nominalists and empiricists, we are led to deny both universals, by our nominalism, and individual substances, by our empiricism.

The English word *substance* comes from the Latin *substans*, which means "stand under"; so substance is that which continues to stand under and support changing accidents, like the same leaf changing its colors, or a balloon being blown up and changing its size. But since all we ever see are the changing accidents, if we are empiricists, substance becomes an unknowable "I know not what." But without substances, nothing remains unchanging, not even the human self, according to Hume. There is only an ongoing stream of accidents and actions, adjectives and verbs with no nouns. Hume, like Buddha, denied the existence of a substantial self or ego. (One wonders, then, just "Hume" he is speaking of when he says "I.")

And this denial of substantial individuality is also reflected in our culture. We experience not only a crisis of universality (because of our nominalism's denial of universals) but also a crisis of individuality and individual identity (because of our empiricism's denial of individual substances). Thus, our identity dissolves into always-changing accidents, attributes, qualities, acts, choices, etc. The self is seen as a "project" or a "construct" rather than as a given reality. The born baby as well as the unborn baby becomes only a "potential person." The consequence of this metaphysic is radical, for if I am not the same person today as I will be tomorrow, then you had better not rely on "my" promises to be faithful. And without promise-keeping, all of society falls apart, beginning with families. Once again we see that the most radical practical consequences for a culture come from changes in its philosophy—most fundamentally its metaphysics.

The two denials, of universality and of individuality, go together, since the universality of essences and the particularity of individual existing substances go together. So when one of these two dies, the other does also—to be replaced by what? In nature, a single random flux onto which we arbitrarily impose our categories. In society, either collectivism and totalitarianism, which has no free individuals, or individualism and libertarianism, which has no solidarity and true community. In the self, either a blind conformism to fashion an ideology or an equally blind absolutizing of freedom and rebellion—or both together.

18

Are Categories Real?

Aristotle said, commonsensically, everything that exists must exist either in itself or in another being. He called the first kind of beings "substances" and the second kind "accidents." He divided "accidents" into nine kinds: qualities, quantities, actions, passions (i.e., receptions, being-acted-upon), times, places, relations, postures (order within internal parts), and possessions. The list may not be the best one (e.g., postures and possessions do not seem as fundamental as the others, and relation seems *more* fundamental than the others); but some similar list of fundamental categories or "the highest general classes of things" seems to be both theoretically necessary and practically useful.

Today most people think of categories as our arbitrarily imposed classes that divide things. We think we can classify things any way we want—for example, into things I'm interested in and things I'm not, or into ducks weighing more than five pounds and all other beings. But Aristotle thought of the fundamental categories as natural, objectively real, and to be discovered by the mind rather than invented and imposed by the will or the feelings.

Of course, there do exist many such arbitrary, willfully created, subjective categories in our thought. The question is whether there are also objective, nonarbitrary categories that are in our thought because they are discovered in reality.

The question is whether nature as well as man has put things in order. Of course, all the natural sciences presuppose the answer is yes.

The question is whether our most fundamental thoughts reflect the most fundamental kinds of things. If so, the order of our subjective intelligence and the order of nature's objective intelligibility are akin and made for each other, like Adam and Eve. If not, if categories are only subjective, if we, not God or nature, invented them all, then that must include the categories of space and time, light and darkness, life and death, good and evil. That philosophy is the death of not only philosophy but also science and common sense.

The impact of this metaphysical issue of the status of categories on theology is immediate and crucial for Christians, because we cannot think clearly and rightly of God or Christ without the categories of "person" and "nature." The God of Christianity is a Trinity of three Persons in a unity of one nature, substance, essence, or being; and the Christ of Christianity is one Person with two natures, human and divine. These are the two most fundamental dogmas of Christianity, and they require categories to state them. Theology is not just psychology; Christianity claims to tell us what God and Christ really are, not merely how Christians have chosen to think about them; and this presupposes a metaphysical realism about categories. Catholics cannot think of the Eucharist without the categories of substance and accidents; or about man without the categories of body and soul, or matter and spirit, or matter and form. It is not the authority of Aristotle that is at issue here but of common sense, of which Aristotle was simply a prophet.

Of course, we can invent any categories we want. That gives us a glorious freedom that cannot be refuted but also cannot discover truth. But real categories are not created by our thought; they judge and limit our thought. And we *want* that, deep down; we want to be limited by truth, by reality, by being. We don't really want to play God and create our own universe. We want truth more than we want freedom—unless our name is Satan, whose philosophy was "Better to reign in hell than serve in heaven."

19

Is Spirit Real?

When determining if spirit is real, we need to define terms clearly first.

Matter means (1) what can be observed with our senses or with the instruments that extend them; (2) what has parts outside of parts; (3) what can therefore be destroyed by removing some necessary parts; (4) what is spatial and therefore can be imagined by the sensory-spatial imagination; and (5) what can be quantified (counted, mathematicized). None of these five things is true of spirit or soul or mind, which are immaterial or nonmaterial. We cannot see spirits; spirits have no parts; they are immortal; they are unimaginable; and they cannot be reduced to quantities, as pictures can be reduced to a number of pixels, and atoms to a number of subatomic particles.

Spirit is not material. The two essential positive qualities or powers of spirit, or mind, are (1) abstract, rational thought and (2) voluntary, free will, or free choice. Atoms don't think or choose; Adams do.

Soul is usually used in ordinary language today as synonymous with *spirit* or *mind*. The older use of *soul* was broader. It meant life, the power of a being to move itself actively, from within. Inorganic chemicals are mere matter, without life; plants, animals, and humans have "souls" in the older, broader sense of the word: plant life, animal life, and human life. Only animals and humans have feelings; and only humans have rational minds and free wills. (Some of our human feelings are shared with animals—for example, pleasure, pain, fear, and desire; others are distinctively human and spiritual—guilt, gratitude, duty, and awe.)

Person is usually used in ordinary language to mean only human persons; but if God or gods or angels exist, they are also persons, since they have minds and wills, even though they do not have material bodies. If there are rational animals on other planets, they, too, are persons, but not biologically human persons.

Materialism is used in two different ways. *Practical* materialism is the pursuit of material goods only, or ranking them more important than spiritual goods in practice, whether or not one believes that there exists also spiritual goods or spiritual things in theory. *Metaphysical* materialism is a philosophical theory that denies that spirit or spiritual things exist at all. It maintains that to be is to be material. Thus, for a materialist either there is no God and no spirit or soul (this is the commonest view among materialists) or, if they exist, they, too, are made of matter (this is the view of Hobbes).

The immediate logical difficulty with metaphysical materialism is that it is self-contradictory because it is an ism, a thought, not a thing thought about. Thought is not made of matter, it is about matter. It is the meaning of matter, as the concept *duck* is not itself a duck; it intends or knows a duck. The word *duck* is also not a duck; it means a duck.

We all know most thought is *dependent on* matter in that it is conditioned and limited by the material brain. Chemicals or blows inflicted on the body and brain change our thinking. But to say x is *conditioned* by y is not the same as saying x is totally *determined* by y.

And even if thought is totally determined by matter (i.e., caused by matter), that does not mean it is only matter (i.e., made of matter). To be caused by parents is not to be a parent but a child. To be caused by an artist is not to be an artist; it is to be art.

There is scientific, empirical evidence that the material brain does not produce thought but limits it, like a "reducing valve" or a faucet. Electroencephalograms of brains in mystical experience, when the alpha waves (that manifest life and consciousness) are the strongest compared to other states, show the addition of no physical or chemical activity but a subtraction of the brain activities manifested by beta and theta waves.

There is also considerable scientific evidence that in near-death experiences and out-of-body experiences, even when brains are totally dead and inoperative, thought is going on. For instance, there are verified cases of observations of empirical events by brain-dead persons who "come back" and report things going on around them when they were brain-dead.[1]

Materialists often claim they can explain all so-called spiritual things, including mystical experience, mathematical intelligence, moral conscience, and human wisdom, by pointing to a physical and/or chemical event in the brain. And they argue from this fact, coupled with the scientific principle of Ockham's razor (the principle that the simplest explanation that explains all the data should always be preferred to a more complex one), that materialism is correct because it is simpler than a dualism of spirit and matter.

But the immaterialist, who believes everything is spirit and that what seems to be matter is really only mind, can equally argue that he can explain every so-called material thing as being only a thought, since no one can point to a material thing without pointing, which is an expression of thinking. We cannot think the unthinkable! And Ockham's razor favors immaterialism over materialism because thought is simpler than matter because it has no spatial parts. To be material means to have parts outside of parts.

---

1   Raymond Moody, *Life After Life* (San Francisco: HarperOne, 2015).

In fact, there are four explanations concerning matter and mind that all explain all the data of our experience: (1) materialism (everything is matter), (2) immaterialism (everything is spirit or mind), (3) dualism (both mind and matter exist independently and interact causally), and (4) good old Aristotle's common sense hylomorphism (literally, "theory of form and matter together") or what psychologists call our "psychosomatic unity," in which our body and soul are related in the same way as the words and the meaning of a book. Logic may be unable to refute any one of these four explanations, but experience is certainly on the side of Aristotle.

Materialist philosophers include Democritus, Lucretius, Hobbes, and Marx. Immaterialist philosophers include Berkeley, Shankara, and Buddha. Dualists include Plato, Descartes, Malebranche, and al-Ash'arī. Hylomorphists include Aristotle, Aquinas, and Lord Commonsense (who is in hiding in the witness protection program).

The most persuasive argument against materialism is its practical consequences. They are radical, and in Western societies they are seldom lived, but under Communism they were. As the Communist agent tells the naïve Doctor Zhivago, "The personal life is dead in Russia. History has killed it." For if we are merely very complex "machines made of meat," and if soul or spirit is a superstition rather than a reality, then totalitarianism is reasonable, and the appropriate treatment of persons is merely a more complex version of the appropriate treatment of machines. When the Coke machine fails to deliver a Coke, we do not appeal to its conscience or reason with it morally; we kick it, or put new parts in it. This is what is done in *Brave New World*, and the citizen-machines do not rebel because the kicking (the conditioning) is not unpleasant. People are produced in test tubes, totally conditioned, and when they malfunction, they are simply reconditioned—or disposed of, painlessly. *Why not?* How many have a good answer to that question today?

The most common temptation to embrace metaphysical materialism in our culture, as distinct from totalitarian cultures, is not political but scientific. Science has proved itself spectacularly successful in dealing with material—empirical material—so there is a natural temptation to think there ought to be no limits to its success, and there are no such things as "souls" that are beyond its competence.

Without science and its offspring, technology, we would not have millions of cures in hospitals. Nor would we have millions of murders in Auschwitz. It does not take a mystic or a saint to know the most serious problems of human life are the problems physical science cannot solve.

20

Is Change Self-Contradictory?
How Can the Same
Thing Become Different?

Our bodies, including our brains, are in both time and space. Our minds (which use our brains, until we die) are not in space, but they are in time. It takes time to think, even when we think of timeless truths like 2+2=4. Not everything human is spatial, but everything human is temporal. Even thought, though it has no spatial qualities (shape, size, color), has temporal qualities: it takes time, it happens in time, it moves from past to future, and it changes. We change our minds more often than we change our clothes. Even if there are "timeless moments" in human life, moments when time seems to stop, it does not really stop because even these "timeless moments" are moments that must occur in time, at certain times. We can perhaps stop being aware of time, but we cannot stop time itself.

A few philosophers, like Parmenides, have claimed change is not real because it seems to be a logical impossibility, a self-contradiction. If I actually change, that means I am not the same as I was in the past. But if I am not the same, if it is not the same I as it used to be, then it cannot be said it is I who have changed. Parmenides thought time was illogical because it violated the law of identity, that x = x.

Aristotle solved this problem by distinguishing the essential or substantial from the accidental. The same unchanged substance acquires changed accidents. This explains human experience. For instance, in education, this is why we reward the same student (in his substance or essence) for being not the same but better (in the accident of his knowledge) on a retest he passed than on a test he failed. And in surgery, we transplant a new heart or kidney into the same patient who lacked one yesterday, not into another patient.

Aristotle also solved the problem by distinguishing potentiality and actuality as two different modes of being, or ways of being real. The same person who was potentially singing a moment ago is actually singing now.

This is not the most pressing problem in philosophy, but it is a clear illustration of how good philosophy typically works, in the following three steps:

1. Experience plus reflection produces a dilemma. What we seem to know instinctively and experientially and commonsensically seems to conflict with something we seem to know logically.
2. The philosopher takes the question seriously and does not simply dismiss it and prefer common sense. He enters into the debate logically and accepts the principles of logic as well as the data of experience.
3. He explains how what we know by experience does not conflict with logic by making distinctions that were not made before or definitions that were not clear before.

In the present case, Aristotle's distinctions were between essence and accidents, and also between potentiality and actuality. The student was first actually flunking and only potentially passing. Then, by passing the retest, he became actually passing. But it was the same student in essence who changed the accident of the level of his knowledge.

This is not the only strategy for philosophy, but it is a common one. Another one is refutation by reducing one of the two logical possibilities to an absurdity, thereby proving the other. For instance, if change does not really happen, then you cannot expect me to change my mind from my present belief that change does happen to your belief that it does not; so stop arguing.

21

Are There Degrees of Reality?

Is God more real than creatures? Is good more real than evil? Are essences more real than accidents? Is spirit more real than matter? Can a person become more "real"? Are fakes "real"?

Are there only two possibilities: "to be or not to be"? Or are there many degrees of realness? In other words, is being digital or analogical?

If being is analogical, then it is "fuzzy," and there are degrees and differences that cannot be precisely quantified. Qualitative differences cannot be reduced to quantitative differences, as the difference between a beautiful picture and an ugly one cannot be reduced to a number of pixels.

Numbers are totally clear and totally distinct. Two cannot cozy up to three and become a little more three-like. So the question is, Can qualities be quantified? Can a football quarterback's quantitative "quarterback rating" of 125.7 or his IQ of 120 communicate everything in his performance or his intelligence, only more exactly than qualitative terms?

Can moral goodness be quantified? Does God judge the dead by computer logic? Do we get a heavenly "credit score" in numbers from the empyrean Experian?

Aristotle would say no. He distinguishes quality and quantity as two different categories, neither of which can be reduced to the other or be explained as a subset of the other or an application or modification of the other. To try to do so, he says, would commit the fallacy of "going over into another genus." Genera are the fundamentally distinct, irreducibly distinct, categories of being.

And Aristotle also sees "being" itself as a "more or less" rather than a simple "to be or not to be." A substance (e.g., a rose) is more *real*, in a sense, than an accident (e.g., redness). One reason this is true is that substances (e.g., dogs) are more lasting than their changing accidents (e.g., their hair color, size, or appetite). The substance is like a hotel room, and the changing accidents are like guests who enter and exit the room.

Paradoxically, however, it is substances that do change and accidents that don't: it is the leaf that changes from green to red, but greenness does not change to redness.

That sounds like a contradiction, but it is not, because the substance changes in its accidents but not in its essence.

A second reason why a substance is more real than an accident is that a substance is independently real, real in itself, rather than dependently or relatively real, real only as existing in another, in something else, for accidents exist only in substances.

Aquinas adds there is also a difference in degree of being between Creator and creatures. God is more real than creatures because he is the fullness of being. He is infinite, unlimited being rather than being limited by anything. He is also the independently real uncaused cause; everything else is dependently real because it is caused to be, brought into existence by something else. And this is a difference in *being*, a difference between two different ways of having being: God has being eternally and necessarily by his own essence, while creatures have being only because their being is caused by other beings and ultimately by Being Itself.

God is not "a" being, not even "the prime" being, but Being Itself. He is not one among many. He is absolutely unique. Compared with God, creatures are almost nothing.

Good and evil, like light and darkness, also have different degrees of being or kinds of being. Darkness is real, but it is not a substantial reality. It is only the absence of light. And evil is real, but it is not an independent reality; it is a brokenness in a being that is good. Even the devil is ontologically good, good in his being, because God created him, but God did not create the evil in him; that was his own free choice.

So when we become less sinful and more saintly, we become more real, more godlike. For God is the touchstone and standard of reality. Those in hell are not only not as *good* and not as *happy* as those in heaven; they are also not as *real*. (Read C. S. Lewis' *The Great Divorce* for concrete examples of this principle. It's a miniature of Dante's *Divine Comedy*.)

So the answer to our question is yes, being has degrees. "Being" must be analogical, with a range of meanings, rather than univocal, with one and only one meaning—like most important words, like *good* and *true* and *beautiful* and *happy*. In fact, if you don't understand analogy, you don't understand anything at all except numbers, which have no range of meanings, no analogical meanings. In other words, you are a computer.

22

What Is the Connection between Metaphysics and Ethics?

The connection between metaphysics and ethics is like the connection between the foundation and the building. Metaphysics is about what is real, and ethics is about what is good; and if it isn't real, it can't really be good. A good (or an end, or a value, or an ideal) is not worth striving for if it is unreal and impossible.

Also, as we saw in the last chapter, degrees of goodness depend on degrees of being. God is the standard for both goodness and being. The more godlike anything is, the better and more real it is.

But most people don't think ethics has anything to do with metaphysics. For almost everybody has an ethics and thinks ethics is important, but most people don't have a metaphysics or think metaphysics is important.

Well, they're wrong about metaphysics. The most important ethical question, how we should live and what we should live for, depends on the most important metaphysical question, Is there a being greater than ourselves or not? Is there a God? Is the soul immortal? Is there a heaven and a hell? Is there supernatural and superhuman reality or not? If so, it's life's greatest tragedy not to live for it; and if not, it's a waste of time and energy to live for it.

How could it be otherwise? The metaphysical claim about the being or nonbeing of God, or something like God, is like the claim of the firemen in the street below to have a net to catch you if you leap from the twentieth floor of the burning building. If the net does not have real being but is only a dream, you will meet a very different fate after you leap the "leap of faith" than the fate you will meet if it does have real being.

In his autobiography *Surprised by Joy*, C. S. Lewis confesses that before his conversion from atheism to theism, "nearly all that I loved I believed to be imaginary; nearly all that I believed to be real I thought grim and meaningless."

Put in more abstract terms, if the three greatest values, namely, goodness and truth and beauty, are only subjective ideals, and not realities, as Lewis believed before his conversion, then we are in Lewis' dilemma and in a kind of ultimate despair. The alternative is ultimate hope. So the answer to what difference does metaphysics make is, only the difference between hope and despair.

There are four possibilities for both metaphysics and ethics. (1) A materialistic metaphysics naturally entails a materialistic ethics. (2) At the opposite extreme, an immaterialist metaphysics, which denies the reality of matter and material goods, naturally entails an ethics that ignores or despises material goods, even biological life itself. (3) A dualistic metaphysics of matter *versus* spirit naturally entails a dualistic ethics that does not connect or integrate life's material goods with its spiritual goods. (4) And a theistic metaphysics—and especially a Christian, "incarnational" metaphysics, and most especially a Catholic (or Orthodox) "sacramental" metaphysics—affirms, orders, integrates, and hierarchizes all the goods in human life.

Part III

Special Metaphysics: Cosmology

The very word *cosmology* has built into it an assumption that is philosophical and implicitly religious. For what we moderns call simply "the universe" or "the world of nature," the ancients called "the cosmos," which means "the intelligently ordered whole," thereby implying some kind of superhuman intelligent orderer or designer. And, of course, when we call it "the creation," we presuppose a Creator.

Cosmology means literally the science (*logos*) of the cosmos, using *science* in its broad, premodern sense of knowledge ordered by reason—which includes philosophy as well as the special sciences, which use the scientific method. Some of the questions dealt with by philosophical cosmology have been answered by modern science, but not all, as we shall see in this section. Cosmology is not dead in modern philosophy, just skinnier. Thus, this section is shorter than most of the others.

One of the most important questions of cosmology in premodern times that has been definitively settled by modern science is whether the universe had a beginning or was eternal; whether the amount of past time was infinite or finite. The three Western religions, Judaism, Christianity, and Islam, all believed time was finite because an essential part of their faith, their divinely revealed religion, was the doctrine that the universe of matter, time, and space had been created by God.

But could this doctrine of faith be proved by reason? There were three views on this subject. Some philosophers (like Bonaventure) thought natural reason alone, unaided by faith in divine revelation, could also prove logically that the universe had a beginning. Others, like Aquinas, thought it could not be either proved or disproved by philosophical reasoning alone. Still others, like Averroës among Muslim philosophers and Siger of Brabant among Christians, thought reason disproved it; that reason could prove the cosmos was eternal; so if faith required believing it was not, there must be a "double truth," or a truth of reason and a truth of faith, which contradicted each other.

Aquinas opposed the "double truth" view passionately, for both faith and reason were imperiled by it. It implicitly exalted reason to the status of being a judge over the revealed mind of God, reduced the faith to a myth or a "good lie," and reduced God to a teacher who wrote two books that contradicted each other: the book of nature and natural reason on the one hand and the book of Scripture on the other.

When the big bang theory was first proposed, by a Jesuit priest, on the basis of strictly scientific evidence, all unbelieving scientists decried it as smuggling religion into science, or rationalizing a prior prejudice rather than open-minded scientific reasoning. But modern astrophysics has definitively proved the big bang, and the fact that the universe had an absolutely singular beginning. That is not a proof of the existence of God, or of creation out of nothing, but it *is* a proof that the universe has a birth date.

A similar controversy surrounds Darwin's theory of evolution by natural selection. Most Catholic thinkers today believe it is religiously neutral, and religion is neutral to it. Others, mainly Protestant fundamentalists on the one side and "fundamentalist" atheists on the other side, argue that Scripture's teaching about creation and the scientific theory of evolution contradict each other. The Catholic Church has always taught that modern science alone can neither prove nor disprove the existence of God, of the divine act of creation, or of an immortal soul in man. The fossil record seems to be very strong data for biological evolution, but neither God nor souls leave fossils.

23

What Is Man's Relation to Nature?

Man's relation to nature is the most important or "existential" or life-changing question in cosmology.

The very word *nature*, like the word *cosmos*, has philosophical assumptions embedded within it, or within its use. What people today mean by *nature* is usually one of two things: (1) simply the sum total of all the actual beings that are within the universe of space, time, and matter, as distinct from what (if anything) is supernatural, or not within the natural universe; or else (2) that portion of it which has been untouched by human hands—that is, by our art or technology. But what people in premodern cultures meant (or still mean) by *nature* is a real, invisible force, a potency or potentiality, that causes things to act in specific ways in accordance with their nature—for example, it is the nature of fire to heat, plants to grow, birds to fly, and man to reason.

Morality, too, was natural to man to all premodern philosophers except the Sophists. It was not artificial and man-made. Thus, a "natural moral law" morality prevailed in all premodern cultures. This has radically changed. Modern "politically correct" people are no longer allowed to speak of "unnatural" acts, especially since the "sexual revolution."

History and anthropology show us three different answers to the question of man's relationship to the cosmos, or the universe, or "nature" in the modern sense of that word.

1. Ancient civilizations saw themselves embedded in nature, as parts of nature (but not in a purely materialistic sense). Insofar as they distinguished themselves from nature, they tended to have an awe and respect for it, and often worshipped parts of it as haunted or inhabited by gods.

2. Jewish, Christian, and Muslim cultures "demythologized" nature, making it a mere creature or created being, a divine work of art, and forbade the worship of nature or any part of it as idolatry, because they, unlike pagan cultures, had a clear concept of a single God who was not part of nature but its transcendent Creator. This "demythologization" or secularization of nature was one of the two most important sources of modern science, the other being the development of logical and scientific reasoning, especially among the ancient Greek philosophers.

3. The typically modern mind often still respects and values nature for utilitarian, pragmatic reasons of ecology and survival, and sometimes also as an object of aesthetic appreciation, but no longer sees it as something intelligently designed, purposed, or "meant" by a divine mind. It sees nature as a very complex, living machine, or even something less than a machine (since a machine manifests intelligent design): as the random movements of merely material things or particles with no mind, values, or purposes.

Thus, the Christian view of nature stands between the extremes of pagan idolatry and modern reductionism and materialism, between too much and too little.

We moderns typically feel "alienated" from nature. When we look up at the night sky, we feel we are looking "out" from the only meaningful world, the little world of human reason and art, into almost-infinite emptiness. We call it "outer space." The ancients and medievals never used the word *space* that way. *Space* for them was simply a dimension of material things: "extension." Their word for the sky was a word connoting fullness, not emptiness: not *space* but *the heavens* (*caelum*). The heavens were the manifestation and revelation of heaven itself: "The heavens are telling the glory of God" (Ps 19:1). Many pre-Christian myths said the stars were the fires of the gods shining through holes in the curtain of night. Pagans and Christians alike felt not like insiders looking out but as outsiders looking in.

Once the Creator of both man and nature was rejected or forgotten, man and nature were no longer seen to be akin, like brothers and sisters of a common Father. Thus, man was left alone, "lost in the cosmos." When God is no longer our Father, nature is no longer our mother. We are cosmic orphans.

Yet the heart yearns for a fundamentally different relationship to nature, which explains the popularity of books that teach the older notion of nature like the *Tao Te Ching*, and of saints like Francis of Assisi and poets like Wordsworth and Hopkins who manifest the premodern sensibility to nature.

Of course, science can say nothing about this issue. The fact that the scientist has to treat nature only in its empirical and mathematical dimensions does not entail the conclusion that there are no other dimensions. A surgeon operating on his mother has to look on her as his patient, not his mother, and as a broken machine, not as a child of God with an immortal soul, for purposes of the operation. But that does not mean that that is all she is; that is an abstraction from something more fully real and more primordial.

24

Is Causality Real?

The answer to the question of whether causality is real is of course it is, you say. It's common sense. Causality is the fundamental principle of all explanation, both commonsensical and scientific. Nothing comes to be without a cause, and the being in the effect cannot be more than the being in the cause or causes, because nothing can give what it does not have. You can't get something from nothing, or more from less (although "less" can be complex and powerful enough to produce what seems to be a "more" by accretion, growth, or actualization of potentialities).

But philosophers do not always agree with common sense. Hume, the very logical and skeptical "hard empiricist," argued that since we cannot *sense* the causal connection between any two events, causality is not a knowable objective reality but just a mental category we impose upon the events we see. It is only our subjective psychological habit, not nature's objectively real connecting link. We see birds and eggs so often we come to think that birds really *cause* eggs, but it is only the psychological, subjective causality between our repeated seeing and our habitual expectation, not a real, objective causality between real birds and real eggs. (I doubt whether any "deadbeat dad" has used Hume's philosophy in court to disqualify his paternity test.)

But isn't this *psychological* causality, the fact that one idea (the idea of eggs) causes another (the idea of birds) to arise in our mind, also a real fact, a real event, and an example of real causality? Hume replies that one *thought* may indeed cause another thought to exist, and that the experience of repetition *causes* the habit of expectation, but that does not mean that one objectively real thing really causes another thing to exist. Our fundamental mental category cannot be known to correspond to anything in the real world.

This, of course, imperils all rational arguments for God, since causality is the connecting link between the Creator and creatures and therefore the connecting link between our knowledge of creatures and our knowledge of the Creator, as our knowledge of works of art is the link to our knowledge of the existence and nature of the artist. The only two arguments in the Bible for the existence of God are the two causal arguments Saint Paul refers to in Romans 1: the arguments from nature and conscience—that we know God as the only adequate cause and explanation of the existence and order of nature, and also as the only adequate cause and explanation of our absolute obligation to be morally good.

But not only common sense and religion but also science depends on real causality. If causality is only subjective and psychological, all sciences are really divisions of psychology. They tell us only how we think, not how things really are.

Immanuel Kant tried to answer Hume's skepticism by saying that's true of all our knowledge; we do not know things-in-themselves, or objective reality, at all, only our own necessary ways of thinking. The logical consequence of this for metaphysics is that "being" itself is only a mental category, not an objective reality, so being itself is not real! Who can believe that? I Kant. But Kant can. And many other philosophers can, too, and they buy into the assumption that Kant has made traditional objective metaphysics impossible.

As mentioned in the section on epistemology, all forms of skepticism are self-contradictory, including Kant's. Is it a real matter of fact, is it a real thing-in-itself, that we cannot know real matters of fact or things-in-themselves? If so, the claim contradicts itself; if not, it leads to the infinite regress that *that* idea, too (that we cannot know that we cannot know real matters of fact or things-in-themselves) is not a real matter of fact or a thing-in-itself, etc., etc.

Kant is almost universally respected as one of the most important and intelligent philosophers who ever lived. But to be important and to be intelligent are not necessarily the same as to be right.

If causality, like "being," is a mere mental category, then Kant's idea that the cause of our knowledge of causality is psychological rather than ontological (metaphysical) is also a mere mental category, not a real cause.

The contradiction to common sense is massive. If murderers do not really cause murders, then why do we have murder trials? Shouldn't we put the murderer of metaphysics on trial?

25

Are There Four (Kinds of) Causes?

Aristotle gave us a very useful device to explain anything by classifying all the kinds of questions anyone can ever ask about anything into four categories. We can ask (1) *what* a thing is—its nature, or essence; (2) what it is *made of* or made from; (3) what *made* it; or (4) what it is *for*, what its natural end is. The first, he called its "formal cause"; the second, its "material cause"; the third, its "efficient cause"; and the fourth, its "final cause."

For instance, the White House is (1) a house (2) made of wood and metal (3) by carpenters (4) for a family to live in. A human being is a (1) rational (2) animal (3) procreated (4) for a life of love, and ultimately for heaven and for the Beatific Vision of God. A virtue is (1) a morally good (2) habit (3) developed by repeated acts (4) that brings about human happiness and perfection. Laws are (1) ordinances (2) of practical reason (3) made and promulgated by authorities (4) for the common good of a community. A burp is (1) an audible explosion (2) of digestive wind (3) from air pressure in the esophagus (4) to relieve digestive tension.

The Greek word for "causes" (*aities*) means that which accounts for or explains the reality of something; that which is responsible for that something being all that it is; that without which the thing would not be or be what it is. The modern English word *cause* is usually used in a narrower sense, to mean only what Aristotle called the "efficient cause," the agent or origin that brings it into existence or changes its state once it exists.

The "efficient cause" is the push, and the "final cause" is the pull. When a man courts a woman, his love is the efficient cause, and her beauty is the objective final cause, and his hope to marry her is the subjective final cause.

The four causes are a very useful way of classifying questions and answers, or explanations. A complete explanation requires all four causes. The formal and material causes are the two aspects or dimensions of a thing's own inner being; the efficient and final cause are the two forces or factors outside the thing that account for it: the "before" and the "after," so to speak.

For Aristotle, the rational soul is the form or formal cause, and the animal body is the material cause, of man. They are not two beings or entities or substances but two dimensions of one substance, like the words (which are the matter) and the message or meaning (which is the form) of a book, or the sounds (matter) and the beauty (form) of a piece of music. To change one is always to change the other. "Form" here means not external shape but internal essence.

Modern philosophy tends to doubt formal and final causes. We dealt with the formal cause in the section on metaphysics, in the chapters about universals and essences. We deal here, in the next question, with the final cause.

26

Are Final Causes (Teleology) Real?

Obviously, final causes (teleology) are subjectively real. Human beings do things for consciously chosen purposes, as means to a desired end. But does all of nature also act for an end, unconsciously? That is the question of teleology (from the Greek word *telos*, meaning end or goal). The main reason the question is controversial is that teleology seems to imply intelligent design. For purposes do not just *happen*, like storms; they presuppose a purposer, so if there is design in the cosmos, there is a cosmic Designer, and that sounds like a God.

Thus, atheists escape the "design argument" for God by insisting that when we speak of teleology or purpose in nature, we are only projecting our own experience of conscious designing and purposing out onto nature, which really has no mind either in it or behind it, and therefore no purpose.

But a thing without mind in it can still have an end or purpose and a mind behind it, like an arrow directed to a target or a saddle designed to hold a person on a horse. Of course, subhuman nature does not think, but its Creator and Designer does. The universe does not have to be an artist in order for it to be a work of art.

And it *is* a work of art, of the highest brilliance and beauty, as any great scientist knows. It is something far more complexly ordered and beautiful than we could ever design.

The teleological argument can move either way: from artist to art or from art to artist. One can argue from a God to a cosmic teleology, down or forward, so to speak, from the cause to the effect; or one can argue upward or backward from cosmic teleology to a God. We could argue from Designer to design or from design to Designer; from cause to effect or from effect to cause. The first argument is theological, assuming the reality of God; the second is philosophical, beginning with creatures. That is the design argument for God.

So what is the rational evidence for objective teleology in creatures that makes the philosophical design argument for God seem to work? What reasons do we have, apart from a prior belief in God, for thinking that nature is teleological, that Aristotle's fourth kind of cause is objectively real?

The answer is very simple. All things in nature change and move, like cars moving down highways. The efficient cause provides only the motor, so to speak, the power or *energy* for the movement, but not the *direction*, the road map, or the destination. It is a matter of empirical observation that things do not just move but move in determinate, specified directions to natural ends. Puppies become dogs, not cats; kittens become cats, not dogs. Acorns become oak trees, not tulips; tulip bulbs become tulips, not oak trees. Electrons move toward protons and away from other electrons. And all masses of matter move toward all other masses of matter and away from antimatter.

Our data is the universe, which is a very long, complex, and gradual evolutionary development of the elements, galaxies, stars, planets, animals, and eventually man out of the raw matter/energy of the universe that appeared suddenly in the big bang. This data can be understood in two opposite ways: either (1) as a nonteleological, merely mechanistic process without any intelligence, design, or teleology, as a mere "push" without any "pull" or end or natural direction, or (2) as a cosmos-wide net of empirical evidence for a designing Mind that does have predestining purposes which explain the *direction* evolution takes. Some see order in nature as caused by disorder, and others see the disorder as part of the order (like a roulette wheel) or as moving in an ordered way toward more order. The evolution of the universe and of life can be seen either way. Is there a good reason, apart from religious faith, for preferring the teleological alternative?

For this is not a matter of faith alone but of reason. Many agnostic or religiously unorthodox scientists (Einstein, for example), who accept nothing by faith, deduce a super-human Mind from two aspects of the universe: (a) from the incredibly precise "fine tuning" of the universe as the "formal cause" or design behind the basic laws of physics, and (b) also from the immensely large set of immensely varied windows of immensely tiny opportunities for human life (the "final cause") to appear. This latter is called "the anthropic principle." A special data base is genetics. DNA appears like an enormously detailed library or instructions.

This all seems to be a rational argument for the common doctrine of all religions, that there is a superhuman Mind. The principle of causality says more cannot come from less, so how can order come from disorder? How can there be design without a Designer?

Atheists have to believe something comes from nothing in two senses: first, in efficient causality (a big bang without a Big Banger), and second, in final and formal causality (a design without a Designer). If there is no final causality in the mindless cosmos that gave birth to us, how can there be final causality in our behavior and our minds? Consistent atheists usually reply that there isn't; the apparently free and rational human love we think is something more than the prehuman matter the prehuman cosmos contains is really only a complex form of animal instinct, and ultimately, of the random movement of blind matter that evolved into animals. That may or may not be logically defensible, but it is not humanly defensible to any human being who has ever loved another. Romeo does not say to Juliet, "My DNA is predestined to be attracted to yours."

Love itself is the highest example of teleology. Animals can love, but only selfishly, from themselves, only out of their own need and instinct. But humans love also for intelligently understood and freely chosen purposes or ends, which include the happiness of the other, the beloved. Animal teleology is only from inside out, from their own desires and needs; human teleology is also from outside in: a response to the aesthetically beautiful or the morally good, to duty, to ideals. Man is more than an animal, and what is more cannot be reduced to what is less, either in the cosmos or in human life.

The question of our relation to the universe is the question of whether our distinctively human goods, values, goals, ideals, and loves "fit" the rest of the universe, at least by analogy. Are there subhuman forms of wisdom and love all the way down, through higher and lower animals, plants, and even subatomic particles? Does something like love go all the way down into the nature of things so that electromagnetic attraction is "love among the particles" and gravity is "the love that moves the sun and the other stars"? And does love go all the way up to the nature of the Creator?

Ultimately the answer to this question depends on whether man and nature are creatures of the same Creator, children of the same Father, works of art of the same Artist. If so, nature is our little sister, and we can speak of even distinctively human morality as a "*natural* law." If not, our position is either that of materialism, which denies the existence of mind (see chapter 19) or that of alienation; we are minds mindlessly produced by a mindless material machine, ghosts haunting a large haunted house called the universe. In that case we are "spiritual but not religious" in a universe that is neither.

27

Is Time Real?

Of course, we all know time is real, but some philosophers say it isn't, for three very different reasons.

1. Some are rationalists like Parmenides who see time and change as logically self-contradictory.
2. Others are more mystical and say true reality transcends ordinary consciousness, which is temporal. They say we are like ants crawling across a painting. The painting is complete and timeless in itself. We are seeing it in the only way the ants can, bit by bit.
3. Others, like Kant, say time is only our universal and necessary but subjective way of organizing things, rather than a known objective reality, a thing-in-itself outside our consciousness.

We have dealt with the first reason, Parmenides' denial of time already in chapter 20; and with the third reason, Kant's belief that we do not know objective reality but construct it in the very act of knowing, in chapter 9. What of the second reason, the mystical notion that true being is eternal and timeless?

The mystical denial of the reality of time usually says it is impossible for us to see this truth unless we transcend reason into mystical experience. But sometimes the mystic gives a rational theological argument for this denial of time, and philosophy can refute this argument. The argument is that God, who is the standard of reality, is timeless, and his mind is timeless, and he sees everything as it truly is, and he sees it all at once and all together (though perfectly ordered) in his timeless present, so the closer we get to that divine standard for reality and truth, the truer our thought is. Therefore, the truest account of time is that it is timelessness, not time, that is real.

The answer is simply that what God creates is real, and God created time, so time is real.

So divine revelation settles the question, even if philosophy does not. Time must be metaphysically real because time is a dimension of the universe that God really created and made to be metaphysically real. The doctrine of creation affirms that the finite and temporal universe God created is not just his dream, as in some forms of Hinduism; it is his creation. It exists, even though it is not God, just as we exist, even though we are not God. (Hope you were not too shocked by that sudden revelation.)

However, the *nature* of time is a tricky question.

Most languages have two words for time: in Greek, *kronos* means the time that measures material motion through space and thus presupposes matter and space, while *kairos* means the time that measures the changes in mind and will or purpose. *Kairos* is "spiritual time." It is a dimension of angelic existence (angels are pure spirits), so it could be said to be cocreated with angels. In a parallel way, *kronos* is a dimension of material existence, and so it could be said to be cocreated with the material universe. Thus, *kronos* has a materially measurable beginning and duration: it began some fourteen billion years ago in the big bang. *Kairos*, too, has a beginning (it is created), but that beginning is not measurable in material time. The movement of matter in the universe cannot date the creation of the universe of angels, only of the material universe.

Angels are more like God than like matter in that they are purely spiritual. But they are more like matter than like God in that they, unlike God, are created, and also in that they have a before and an after, a past and a future, because even though they do not have *kronos*, they do have *kairos*, while God is timeless.

Man, who is material and spiritual, is part of both universes—matter and spirit, *kronos* and *kairos*. He has *kairos* because he has a spiritual soul, and he has *kronos* because he has a material body. Once the body dies, the soul is no longer in the body and in the material universe and in *kronos*; thus our time in purgatory or heaven cannot be measured by chronometers.

Pagan Greek philosophers believed past time was infinite; the universe was coeternal with its makers or Maker, with the gods or God. No pagan philosopher ever came up with the idea of a God who created time itself and who created the entire universe out of nothing.

Theists (Jews, Christians, and Muslims) knew past time was finite because the doctrine of creation is part of their "deposit of faith" or divine revelation. Some theists, like Saint Bonaventure, believed this fact (that the extent of past time was finite) could also be proved by reason alone; others, like Aquinas, thought it could not. Modern science, of course, has settled this question through big bang cosmology, which all scientists accept. The universe is only thirteen to fourteen billion years old. Still only a teen.

There are many philosophical paradoxes about time, such as the one Augustine raised, namely, that if the present moment of time is like a point on a line, something that has no length and is only the dividing point between past time and future time, which do have length—if this is the correct view of time, then all three moments of time, the past and the present and the future, seem to disappear into unreality because the present has no length at all. The past is no longer, and the future is not yet. So that spatial analogy of point and line cannot be the correct view of time.

What is the alternative? The present is not a mere point of division between past and future time; and in fact it is the only dimension of time that is actually real. The future is *potentially* real and the past *was* real, but it is the actual, living present that is the time dimension that gives reality to the pastness of the past (by present remembering) and to the futureness of the future (by present anticipating and desiring). For without present memory, the past could not be said to be *past*; and without present anticipation, desire, or fear, the future could not be said to be *future*.

If the present is the dimension of time that is actually real, and if it is "where" (to use a spatial analogy) the meeting or touching between time and eternity (God) happens, then we touch eternity or are touched by it whenever we know eternal truths or are aware of eternal goods and duties, and whenever we pray. We are like Adam's finger being touched by God's finger in the Michelangelo painting on the ceiling of the Sistine Chapel.

Notice the connection between the three meanings of "present": (1) God is present, not absent; (2) he presents himself—that is, he actively gives himself to his creatures like a Christmas present; he is not withheld; and (3) he lives in the present moment, not the dead past or the unborn future. Brother Lawrence, in *The Practice of the Presence of God*, speaks of "the sacrament of the present moment." He calls the present moment a sacrament, or a holy thing, because the present moment is to time what the Eucharist, the Body of Christ, is to matter. (Take "time" to think about that analogy for a moment—that is, for the present moment.)

28

Is Hierarchy Real?

If there is a single philosophical idea that all premodern cos-
mologies accepted and that all or nearly all modern cosmol-
ogies reject, it is the idea of hierarchy, or "the great chain
of being"—that nature is ordered into qualitatively, and not
just quantitatively, different levels: humans over animals, animals over plants, plants over nonliving things. Many modern
philosophers reduce all qualitative differences to quantitative
differences among atoms or subatomic particles.

The most typically modern ethics conforms to this modern cosmology in its attack on all hierarchies or aristocracies
of superiority, which are the metaphysical and cosmological
basis for the traditional ethic of authority and obedience—two
ideas that have become radically misunderstood and reduced
to oppressive power ("might makes right") and slavish conformity that is in need of liberation. Modern politics is egalitarian
and democratic rather than authoritarian and aristocratic: no
kings or queens, only elected representatives. Modern democracy tends to base right (law) on quantitative might: the will
of the majority is the supreme authority. American democracy
is an exception; it explicitly originates in the opposite philosophy, in a rule of law, not of will, of "natural law," the laws not
of man but of "nature and nature's God." But this foundation
is increasingly eroding.

The consequences for religion of this antihierarchical egalitarianism are obvious: the most "out-of-date" institution

in the world, the primary enemy of modern egalitarianism, is the Catholic Church, whose essential claims are all hierarchical. (We speak of *metaphysical* hierarchy here, not merely the hierarchy of ranks with the clergy or of a distinction between clergy and laity.) The Church is not a democracy: God is the absolute authority, and he has established subordinate authorities—angels, apostles, bishops (their successors), popes, pastors and preachers, and saints. What the critics forget is this is a hierarchy of service, not power; the supreme authority on earth is the Christ who "came not to be served but to serve" (Mt 20:28).

The charge is often made that the Church, and all premodern cultures, simply projected their political preferences for hierarchy and monarchy into the cosmos, and that is the origin of not only the cosmological idea of hierarchy but of religion itself and of the idea of God, the King of the universe. But that projection argument is no stronger than its opposite, that the modern mind simply projects *its* political preference for democracy into the cosmos; that its political egalitarianism is the psychological origin of its metaphysical or cosmological egalitarianism. Thus, the issue is left undecided: Is God really superior to man, saints to sinners, and men to animals?

If you don't believe humans are really superior to animals, I will not choose to eat at your house because if you practice your philosophy, you must be either a vegetarian or a cannibal. I like to eat meat and not be meat. And I do not believe "you are what you eat." Bacon does not make me oink.

There are natural and unnatural aristocracies. A wise and just ruler is naturally superior at ruling, superior by right; a foolish and wicked ruler is only superior by might. *Aristocracy* means, literally, "rule based on excellence," not mere superiority of power or wealth or ancestry.

The hierarchy of authority and obedience do not necessarily connote a hierarchy and inequality of value. Within God, or Ultimate Reality, the Son obeys the Father's authority, yet he is equal in all things to the Father. Citizens, children, and wives are equal in value to kings, parents, and husbands, yet they have different roles, different kinds of authority, and different kinds of subordinations. Saint Joseph was radically inferior to both his wife and their son, yet he was the father of the holy family and the one who was most responsible for it. He led them into Egypt and taught his son how to speak, how to work, and how to obey (Lk 2:51).

In the Bible, God is often said to turn human order upside down. In many of the psalms and prophets, and in Mary's Magnificat (Lk 1:46–55) he makes the last (the poor, the humble) to become first and the first (the rich, the proud) to become last; but he does not homogenize them. He changes unnatural and false hierarchies into natural and true ones.

The total attack against hierarchy itself, and against the idea of any real superiority and inferiority, is intrinsically self-contradictory, for it assumes a hierarchy that makes egalitarianism *superior* to aristocracy.

Some philosophers go so far as to assert that the idea of an objective universal truth is itself an oppressive superstition, and they attack logocentrism, or "truth-ism." This attack is central to deconstructionism. But either this attack on truth is put forth as the preferable "truth," and thus is self-contradictory, or else it amounts to no more than the triumph of raw power over reason, justice, and nature, so it is a raging wild beast rather than a philosophy.

The envy or resentment against all hierarchies of intrinsic excellence infects all modern life and institutions. It infects economics in Marxist class envy of the have-nots against the haves, disguised as justice or compassion. It even infects sex and all intrinsic, natural, and divinely ordained sexual differences.

This attack on all "discrimination" is an attempt to undo the essential principle of order in creation. In Genesis 1, for

God to create is to discriminate. He discriminates being from nonbeing, light from darkness, the "waters below" (the earth) from "the waters above" (the heavens), land from sea, living from nonliving, animals from plants, species from species, and then, within our species, men and women, equally but differently made in his image. (For not all natural differences are differences in intrinsic value: a simple point that egalitarians usually forget.) And then the rest of the Bible tirelessly repeats the application of this hierarchical principle to human life and actions in its morally aristocratic philosophy of the hierarchical superiority of good over evil, saints over sinners.

The modern attacker on all discrimination does not discriminate between natural and right discrimination (what God does) and unnatural and wrong discrimination (what man does—for example, racism).

That attack on all natural hierarchies is an attack on the essential principle of the divinely designed order of nature itself; and if that attack is not the supernatural strategy of Satan, then nothing is. Its total success would be total entropy, the homogenization of all energy in the universe, as well as the equation of good with evil, God with the devil. It would abolish adoration.

29

Is Evolution Real?

Evolution can mean four different things: (1) any gradual development; (2) any gradual development toward the good, any progress; (3) Darwin's biological theory of the evolution of new species (macroevolution, as distinct from microevolution within a species) by the mechanism of "natural selection"; or (4) Darwin's atheistic philosophy, which eliminates divine design and claims random chance is sufficient to explain the evolution of species.

I address only the third meaning, for the first two are obviously true in many fields and the fourth is known to be certainly false by all who believe in a divine Creator.

Evolution (sense 3) is a scientific theory; but atheism (4) is not a scientific theory at all, for science can neither prove nor disprove God by the scientific method. We cannot perform controlled experiments on our Creator. Hamlet can choose to believe or not to believe in Shakespeare, but unless Shakespeare puts himself into his own drama (which God actually did, according to Christianity), Hamlet cannot do to Shakespeare what Shakespeare can do to Hamlet.

There is impressive evidence for the theory of evolution in the totality of the fossil record and its chronological order. It is a theory, not an empirical fact, but no other theory explains nearly as much of the factual data. There are unanswered questions and problems about details of the theory, but nothing to simply refute it as a whole. And the only alternative theory, the direct divine creation of each species, (a) has little or no evidence, (b) leaves many more questions unanswered, and, above all, (c) seems inconsistent with God's usual strategy regarding natural events, namely, a reduction of supernatural, miraculous intervention to a minimum and the delegation of power to the agents and agencies he created in the beginning.

This point was made by a number of premodern Christian theologians such as Augustine, who saw the universe as a kind of field in which God planted "seeds" to later grow, and by Aquinas' very basic theological principle that divine grace typically uses and perfects nature and natural causality rather than bypassing it.

The apparent conflict between creationism and evolutionism centers on man, and on that which is distinctive in man—the spiritual, rational, and immortal soul. Souls leave no fossils, so there is no evidence that scientifically proves or disproves the assertion that God directly and supernaturally creates each human soul. There are only religious claims and philosophical arguments, not empirical data, as there is with bodies. The scientific theory of evolution no more proves or disproves souls than it proves or disproves God.

Concerning the origin of the human body, the Genesis account does not use the Hebrew word for "create" (*bara'*) for God's production of the human body but says he made it "of dust from the ground" (Gen 2:7). So the Bible does not either teach or refute the idea of an evolutionary origin of the human body, but it suggests something like it.

In contrast, regarding the spiritual soul, it says God "breathed into his nostrils the breath [or spirit, *ruah'*] of life" and made man "in his own image" (Gen 2:7; 1:27).

But the theory of evolution, insofar as it remains scientific rather than theological, says nothing about the human soul. Souls leave no fossils. There are good philosophical arguments for the reality of immaterial souls, but no strictly scientific ones.

So the trillions of tons of ink and paper that have tried to contribute weapons to "the battle between creationism and evolutionism" that is at the heart of the fake "war between science and religion" have not produced a single victory on either side. Neither side has defeated the other. This is a war without a casualty. Some creationists say evolution is a myth, and some evolutionists say creation is a myth, but the real myth is the so-called "war between science and religion" that both sides believe.

30

Is Time Travel Possible?

The question of whether time travel is possible will probably seem not only unusual but flaky and out in left field. It is an assumption of much science fiction but certainly not of science. Yet it is a fascinating philosophical question, even though its answer is very speculative and uncertain.

Philosophy can apparently conclusively disprove one kind of time travel—the kind we find in most movies or science fiction stories—by a very simple and commonsensical logical argument. If I can actually travel into the past physically, and change physical events, then I could go back into a time before I was born and murder my own father. In that case, without my father, who is a necessary cause of my being, I would not have being. But if I did not have being, I could not murder my father. So the idea of that kind of time travel is logically self-contradictory, or self-refuting.

Changing the past physically seems to be logically impossible; but one could think of another kind of time travel that is not physical but only mental, so it could not cause any physical changes. In fact, we actually have a weak form of that kind of time travel; it is called memory, which is mental travel into the past. And we also have a similar time travel into the future, which is called prediction or anticipation. These powers are severely limited, however, because they are apparently dependent on and conditioned by the physical brain, which is in matter and the time that measures matter and its changes through space, which is *kronos* or chronological time. (See chapter 27 above.)

There is, however, another kind of time, *kairos*, the time that measures purpose and meaningful intention. (Purposes exist only where there is understanding and willing, which are acts of the spirit or soul or mind, not of the body, although in us its activity is dependent on and conditioned by the body, brain, and nervous system.) This "spiritual time" might in theory allow for a stronger kind of memory and/or anticipation, and thus for a kind of time travel greater than our present ordinary memories and anticipations. And something like this does seem to exist in certain mystical experiences.

And perhaps there is also evidence for something like this not just in what is usually labeled as mystical experiences but in our power to tell stories, real or fictional, about events in other times than the present; for in doing this we, in a way, transcend our actual present existence and have a kind of out-of-body experience mentally. Someone whose mind and spirit are so immersed in the events of a great book that the reader is sometimes jolted into surprise when he or she closes the book and reenters the "real" world, which often seems harder to believe is real than the world in the story.

There is abundant scientific evidence that out-of-body experiences happen, especially at the moment of anticipated death, or after temporary apparent brain death which is later reversed (near-death experiences). In these, one's past life events often appear with startlingly vivid truth and clarity, in perfect order although taking no time at all to unfold. However, there are no cases in which the present mind or soul or spirit causally *changes* anything in the past, including past thoughts. It only *observes* the past. The events of the past remain past and unalterable.

There is also abundant evidence of mystical states in which time is seemingly suspended. In some primitive cultures this is common rather than exceptional, for example, the Australian Aborigines with their "dream time" or "the dreaming," in which ordinary time is transcended and time radically changes its nature so that one becomes contemporaneous with the archetypical ancestor(s). Something analogous (but not identical) happens in prayer, when the Christ of history, and not just our memory of him, becomes contemporaneous with us, and we with him. And in the Mass his human Body and Blood, shed on the Cross two thousand years ago, become really present to us and even in us when we receive him. It is more than memory. It is a transcendence of time.

If the mind can be separated from the body and then return, as seems to happen in near-death or out-of-body experiences, that mind *might* be able to enter the future and see it without altering it, then return to the present when it reenters its physical, temporal body. This may happen in genuine prophecy, where the eternal God, whose mind contains all events and all times, allows the prophet to know something that is future to the prophet but present to God. This might also be done with the past—as is apparently done in near-death experiences—to make it a *living* past.

The experience of dying and entering an eternal or semi-eternal (or "sempiternal") mode of existence must also change our time experience, since the soul is no longer in the universe, which is the sum total of all matter and its (material) space and its (chronological, *kronos*) time. In Catholic theology, the new body will have the quality of levity after death, which will allow it to move at will through space instantly, akin to the apparently instantaneous movement of a subatomic particle in quantum theory. So, the resurrected soul may be able to do with time what the resurrected body thus does with space. In fact, Saint Padre Pio and other saints who "bilocate" seem to have had something like this power even in this world and in this life: the power to be simultaneously in two places at the same time, which is a kind of time travel, or transcending the laws of ordinary time, as well as space travel, or transcending the laws of ordinary space.

Of course, this is all highly speculative, and it is foolish to claim that time travel is certain or true or even possible. But it is equally foolish to claim it is impossible. The point of this chapter is simply to open our minds to alternative possibilities, not to close the issue but to open it.

31

How Can We Prove the
Uniformity of Nature?

Modern science claims to be based on pure reason, not on any faith that transcends reason and cannot be proved by reason. Modern science is also based on the empirical method of beginning with experience and reasoning inductively from the data of particular concrete examples to general principles that explain these data, testing all theories by the sensory data and by controlled experiment with the material things we know by the senses and by the instruments that extend the senses. This is one of the things that distinguishes modern science from both religion, which is based at least partly on faith, and philosophy, which argues deductively from abstract universal principles to particular concrete cases, as well as inductively from particulars to universals.

Scientists do not usually want to assume or rely on either religion or philosophy. But apparently science has to do that, for there are two assumptions that underlie all scientific reasoning, and they do not come from science itself but from either religious faith or philosophical reasoning. Or perhaps they come simply from common sense.

One of them is the principle of causality: nothing begins to exist or to change without a cause of its existence or change. A more abstract version of this principle is the principle of sufficient reason: all that is objectively real is in principle intelligible to human reason and rational explanation. That is why the critiques of objectively real causality by Hume and Kant are serious challenges to science as well as philosophy.

The other principle underlying all science is the principle of the uniformity of nature: the fundamental laws of nature—such as gravity, relativity, the speed of light, and the convertibility of mass and energy—do not change with time or place; the laws of physics will be the same one thousand years from now as they are now, and they are the same in other parts of the universe as they are in ours. If nature is not uniform, then scientific reasoning cannot give us assured knowledge of the universe, for these laws may cease to be true at some times or places.

Some physical laws do change because they are descriptions of how matter behaves only at some times, especially very shortly after the big bang, when atoms had not yet formed, or before matter congealed to produce gravity waves. But there are other physical laws, such as entropy, that are true at all times.

Following are possible answers to the question of how we can prove the uniformity of nature:

1. The principle of the uniformity of nature need not be proved at all—but thus all of science becomes uncertain and uncritical. This simply gives up.
2. Believing in this principle is a pragmatic, practical necessity, even if it cannot be proved—but that does not satisfy reason; it does not prove the *truth* of the principle. Sometimes lies are more *practical* than truths.
3. It must be assumed by religious faith—but nonreligious scientists need rational proofs. Faith in God's reliability and consistency does justify the principle, but this cannot be expected of all scientists. Science must be based on universal reason, not a particular faith.
4. It is proved inductively. But proving induction inductively is arguing in a circle or begging the question—that

is, assuming the thing you must prove, smuggling your conclusion into your premises.

5. It is proved by deductive reasoning. But if deductive reasoning cannot prove itself either, then this answer is subject to exactly the same begging-the-question critique as the former one.

   (By the way, begging the question does not mean ignoring the question, as nearly everyone now assumes since no one takes a course in practical logic anymore. Nor does it mean posing the question. It means assuming what you need to prove, smuggling the conclusion back into the premise.)

6. It must be assumed by a secular faith, like the more general faith in human reason itself—for reason cannot prove itself, as we have seen earlier (see chapter 6). This makes a kind of universal "common sense faith" the foundation of science. After all, science is only refined common sense, and we all do in fact begin here, with answer 6. Perhaps there is simply no alternative.

32

Is the Universe Real Independent
of Thought?

The question regarding if the universe is real independent of thought may seem absurd, but an increasing number of ordinary people, rather than a few strange philosophers, actually believe the answer to that question is no.

The most popular origin of that no is not a rational argument but faith in pop psychologists and commencement speakers, who are the only people who tell even bigger lies than lawyers and politicians when they repeat the mantra that "You can be whatever you want to be," or "Create your own reality."

If they actually mean what they say, this does not deserve refutation but exorcism or psychoanalysis. The clearest and most radical mark of insanity is a confusion between the two most fundamentally different kinds of reality, namely, the subjective and the objective, or dreams and realities, or what is dependent on our minds and will and what is independent of them. The maximal insanity would be the claim to be the mind of God, the omniscient Designer of the universe. (Thus, logically, if Jesus is not who he claimed to be, he is the most insane lunatic who ever lived. Or, if he didn't actually believe it, the biggest liar. Which of these two hypotheses, if either, explains the data of the Gospels? And if neither, what then?)

A *philosophical* reason for believing the universe is not objectively real but a projection of thought is that we can indeed imagine or conceive things that do not exist, and we can and often do confuse the real and the unreal, either thinking something unreal to be real or thinking something real to be unreal; so why could we not be all doing this all the time with the universe? It is logically possible—it does not violate the law of noncontradiction—so how do we know it is not true?

That question is similar to the one in the previous chapter—about how we know the principle of the uniformity of nature—and the possible answers to it are similar to those listed there.

Bishop Berkeley tried to prove the material universe did not exist outside minds (either ours or God's). One of his arguments was that it was a logical contradiction for us to *think* a thing still exists when we do *not think* it. But this is a grammatical fallacy, an amphiboly. The adverbial phrase *when we do not think it* may modify the verb *think* or the verb *exists*. It is indeed self-contradictory to think when we do not think, but it is not self-contradictory to think something exists when we are not thinking about it.

Yet when we try to prove the objective existence of the universe by an indubitable rational argument, we may find it much more difficult than we think. The immaterialist has answers to all our objections. For instance, we may object that if matter were merely our own mental projection, we would never have to die or endure pains. But perhaps those evils are simply parts of the mental story we are inventing or the dream we are dreaming, even against our will. Perhaps there is a subconscious will as well as a subconscious mind, and perhaps the relation between our mind and our will is not what our mind thinks it is. Perhaps the subconscious will, which wills these evils, is manipulating the conscious mind, which does not will them. The philosopher Arthur Schopenhauer seems to have believed something like that.

A more likely "perhaps" is that perhaps the more absurd the philosophy seems (like this one), the more we see the need for common sense as a limit and touchstone to philosophical reason.

Yet even apparently absurd and extreme philosophies like immaterialism (the denial of the objective existence of matter and the material universe) can be reminders of a truth that is closer to this absurd idealist extreme than we usually think. For instance, the mental and spiritual factors, faith and will, decide the outcome of wars more decisively than the material factors. Despite immense superiority in technology, the same America that won two wars against its most militarily superior opponents—namely, the Revolutionary War against England and World War II against Germany and Japan—also lost the two wars it fought against its two weakest opponents—North Vietnam and Afghanistan. Similarly, the mental and moral superiority of Greece defeated the vastly greater material superiority of Persia. Hobbits like Frodo and Sam can destroy wizards like Sauron. Christ the Hobbit overcame and trans-formed the world's greatest empire, Rome. And remember that Socrates taught implicitly what Christ taught explicitly: "What shall it profit a man, if he shall gain the whole world, and lose his own soul?" (Mk 8:36, KJV).

Part IV

Special Metaphysics: God

Aristotle distinguished two meanings of metaphysics (which he called simply "first philosophy"): the study of being as such, or being in general, and the study of the first being, or the first cause, or the supreme being. He deduced, by reason alone, many of the attributes of God: oneness, eternity, perfection, necessity (versus contingency or dependence), pure actuality (versus potentiality for change), and "thought thinking itself." Much more is revealed about God by the faith (i.e., the content of divine revelation). But philosophical reason alone can demonstrate that none of the things in the faith that cannot be understood, discovered, or proved by reason (e.g., the Trinity or the Incarnation) ever *contradict* reason. The "God" known by philosophical reason is only a very thin slice of the "God" known by faith in God's own self-revelation, but it is a precious "thin slice." Both the pagan Aristotle and the Christian Saint Thomas Aquinas said even the smallest and most imperfect knowledge of the greatest and most perfect things (the things of God) is more valuable, brings us more perfection, and makes us more deeply happy than the greatest and most perfect knowledge of the smallest things (the things of the world).[1]

---

1   Saint Thomas Aquinas, *Summa Theologica* I, q. 1, a. 5 ad. 1, referencing Aristotle, *De Partibus Animalium*, bk. 1, ch. 5.

33

Is God Real?

Can you prove God exists? If the question means the questioner begins with a concept of God he derived from faith and then is asking whether reason alone can prove the real existence of the being designated by that concept, the answer is clearly no. How could our reason prove what depends on God's will—namely, God's free choice to love us or to create the universe? How could human reason alone know the eternal inner life of God?

Especially if that life is Trinitarian. No strictly rational proof of the Trinity has ever been given. However, all objections to that doctrine can be answered (e.g., oneness and threeness in nature or in person contradict each other, but oneness in nature and threeness in person do not). And Trinitarian clues, analogies, echoes, or reflections abound in the universe and the human soul. But these are not proofs.

But there are literally dozens of good, strictly rational arguments for the existence of a God—that is, a being that has some distinctively divine attributes. These arguments begin not with any faith but only with common human experience, both our experience of the objective world without that we know with our senses (e.g., arguments from the causal contingency and order we find in the universe) and our experience of the subjective world within (e.g., our minds' knowledge of eternal truths and our conscience's experience of absolute moral obligation). Beginning with these premises, the arguments then logically demonstrate that these data can be explained adequately only by the existence of a being with at least some of the attributes that only a being that deserves the name "God" can have. (The first set of arguments are cosmological arguments and the second psychological arguments.)

The most famous versions of the cosmological argument are Saint Thomas Aquinas' five variations on the causal argument: that the existence of (1) change, (2) causal dependence, (3) contingency (potentiality to not exist), (4) degrees of perfection, and (5) teleological order can be explained only by (1) a first, unchanged changer, (2) an uncaused cause of existence, (3) a noncontingent "necessary being," (4) a really perfect being that is the standard for degrees of perfection, and (5) a designing Mind behind teleological design of order-to-an-end. The fifth argument is almost universally understood by cultures that live with nature instead of technology.

Following are the most famous versions of the psychological argument:

1. Augustine's argument from the eternity of knowable truths (like 2+3=5, or Platonic forms like perfect justice) to an eternal Mind in which these truths must reside. (Atheists like Sartre help theists to understand this argument when they argue "there can be no eternal truth because there is no eternal mind to think it.")

2. The moral argument from an objective moral law to a Lawgiver (cf. the beginning of C. S. Lewis' *Mere Christianity*); or Newman's version of the moral argument that does not assume an objective moral law but only the absoluteness of the moral authority of individual conscience, which cannot be dependent on anything with less authority, such as parents or teachers, society's consensus, others' will or opinions, or feelings. Why treat conscience as a divine prophet if there is nothing divine?

3. There is also the psychological argument that faith naturally leads to sanctity and joy. How could the human heart be so badly designed that the two things it wants and needs the most are mutually exclusive and contradictory? These two things are truth on the one hand and on the other hand goodness and altruistic love and the deep joy this brings. Are the great saints or the great sinners the greatest fools? The most effective argument for God has always been saints. They, not philosophers, converted the hard-nosed Roman world.

4. There is also Pascal's pragmatic argument, the "wager," which seeks not to prove that God exists but that belief in God is the world's best "bet" since even if God's existence cannot be proved, it cannot be disproved either, and by the wager or leap of faith, you cannot lose anything and you can gain everything: eternal life.

Other arguments exist, but they are usually more abstract. For example, Saint Anselm's famous ontological argument begins with no premises at all except the definition of God as that "than which nothing greater can be conceived"[1] and then argues that if God lacks real existence, then the God already admitted to be that than which nothing greater can be conceived (that is, possessing all conceivable perfections) is said to be lacking in one conceivable perfection—namely, real existence independent of our minds; so atheism is logically self-contradictory.

The hidden and questionable premise of that argument is that existence is a perfection like wisdom, power, or goodness. But this confuses existence with essence. So Thomists, who accept Saint Thomas' signature teaching of the real distinction between existence and essence, and who are also empiricists, reject Anselm's argument, while essentialists and rationalists like Descartes, Spinoza, Leibnitz, and Hegel accept it.

---

1   Saint Anselm, *Proslogium*, ch. 3.

For Christians, the definitive argument for God's existence is Christ himself. "What think you of God?" is best tested by "What think you of Christ?" (cf. Mt 22:42). If God does not exist, then Christ was very far from being a wise man: he was the most seriously deluded thinker who ever lived. Was Christ the Word (i.e., the revelation) of God, the word of truth, or was he the word (the revelation) of insanity?

If God is as imaginary as Harvey, the mythical giant invisible rabbit in the old Jimmy Stewart movie, then all believers are as nuts as Jimmy Stewart was supposed to be, who still believes in him, and all the saints, sages, and mystics are only overgrown two-year-olds playing a silly infant's game, while it is the atheists like Machiavelli, Marx, Stalin, Mussolini, Hitler, Mao Zedong, Pol Pot, Nietzsche, and Sartre who are the truly wise.

34

What Is God? Who Is God?

When Thomas Aquinas was four, he asked his teacher, "What is God?" Because the teacher's answer did not satisfy him, he became the greatest theologian who ever lived.

And, more importantly, he became *Saint* Thomas. For a saint is a lover, and love is the most necessary cause of understanding persons; that is why saints understand God better than theologians do. Psychologists may understand more *truths about* persons than most persons do, but only persons—that is, beings capable of love—can understand persons themselves.

Reason alone, philosophy alone, without divine revelation, is obviously inadequate to give a complete answer to the question, What is God? It is like a flea trying to understand a dog. This is one reason why the notion of a divine revelation is fitting: the more real a thing is, the more it has to act to reveal itself to us. Numbers are only mental abstractions, not substances or things; and they do not act; they are static. Rocks are not alive, but their concrete presence can act on us and change our lives a little when they block our way. Plants are active from within (that is what it means to have life), and we can understand and predict them fairly well, but not as exactly as rocks. Animals are even more active, and to understand higher animals, we are much more dependent on their revealing themselves to us. When it comes to understanding each other, the activity demanded of the revealer and the revealed-to is roughly equal, except when dealing with the relation between adults and small children, where the activity is unequal. So when dealing with God, who (if he deserves the name at all) is far more superior to us than we are to small children or animals), most or all of the activity must come from God's side. Thus divine revelation.

But human reason alone without divine revelation can give *some* answers, in fact enough to change one's life. If God is the perfect being, the standard of all perfection, then God cannot lack any conceivable perfection. That God is that "than which nothing greater can be conceived"[1] is not a positive definition of God, but it is a good negative one. Saint Anselm used it in his ontological argument, and even though the argument may fail to prove God's existence, there is nothing wrong with the definition with which it begins.

Three of the attributes a perfect being must have without limit are knowledge, goodness, and power; thus God is omniscient (all-knowing), omnibenevolent (all-good), and omnipotent (all-powerful). Knowledge means first of all understanding. Goodness, in persons, means most especially goodwill, which is the will to the best good of the other person, which is the definition of what Scripture and Christ mean by *love* (*agape*). And power means the ability to attain whatever good is known and loved.

What logically follows from these three minimum divine attributes—in other words, the necessary logical consequence of rejecting atheism—is the sentence that can change one's entire life and one's attitude toward one's life: "God works for good with those who love him [i.e., who will his will]" (Rom 8:28). This is a strenuous stretch of faith, a test of faith, a challenge to faith, because it is far from obviously true; in fact it is startling, and there is abundant evidence against it—namely, "the problem of evil." If God is good, why does he allow so

---

1   Saint Anselm, *Proslogium*, ch. 3.

many evils? Yet the startling claim of Romans 8:28 logically and necessarily follows from the premise of the three most nonnegotiable answers to the question, What is the nature of God? A God who is stupid, wicked, or weak does not deserve the name of God.

Other divine attributes can also be logically proved by deduction from this definition, such as God's eternity. If God's goodness is unlimited, it cannot change from anything worse or *to* anything worse.

Also, unity. There cannot be two Gods because if God is perfect and has only perfections and not imperfections, then some perfection must distinguish one of these two Gods from the other, and whichever of the two lacks that perfection is not totally perfect and thus not a God.

Also, if God is all-good, he must be all-just. What about mercy? If mercy is a relaxation of justice, God cannot have mercy. But even among us, mercy is a perfection. Therefore mercy cannot be a relaxation of justice but must presuppose justice and go beyond it in moral perfection. Thus, we see how reasoning theologically about the nature of God can have practical moral consequences for human life and action.

For God to create us cannot be due to justice, for a being that does not even exist yet cannot deserve anything, not even existence. So it must be due to something more than justice, something more like mercy or sheer generosity.

But whatever depends on God's free choice cannot be logically deduced. Thus, God's choice to create us, to forgive us, to redeem us, to glorify us, and to providentially care for every aspect of our humble lives cannot be strictly deduced. However, all objections to it can be answered. For example, it is not an imperfection to care for humble and unworthy things and persons as well as worthy ones.

God did not have to create cats, either tigers or kittens—it was his free choice—so they cannot be deduced from God's nature. Nor can angels. But once cats exist, we can see their rational coherence with an all-perfect God, whose perfections include unpredictable creativity and incredible generosity. And we can also demonstrate by reason that angels are possible, and even likely, and that they probably exist in immense kinds and ranks, since they fill the gap between us and God, just as many species of animals fill the gap between us and plants. If God is so creative that he invents cats and puffer fish, he can invent angels too. These are not proofs but "arguments from fittingness," a category the medievals loved to use but which the modern mind distrusts because it is much more appropriate in art than in science. But is the universe a machine or a work of art? And the same question applies to us.

The two answers to the question—How much can we prove by reason alone about the nature of God?—that are certainly wrong are everything and nothing. For the two classes of truths—truths known by faith and truths known by reason—are neither identical (the everything answer) nor mutually exclusive (the nothing answer) but partially overlapping. The "thin slice" of God that philosophical reason can know is a part of the "thick slice" of God that we know by faith in divine revelation through Christ, his Church, and her Scriptures. Just how large that "thin slice" is, is a matter of some legitimate dispute and uncertainty.

35

How Can We Know God?

The question regarding how we can know God is not whether we can, because we do. The previous two chapters tried to show that. But how? How is it possible?

First of all, we must distinguish two kinds of knowing: (1) the concrete, involved, experiential, practical knowing with which we know each other and the things in our lives (*kennen, connaitre*) and (2) the abstract, detached, scientific, theoretical knowing of truths *about* persons and things (*wissen, savoir*). We have a real but imperfect knowledge of God in both ways.

We know God in the first sense (*kennen*) in at least eight ways: (1) through prayer; (2) through genuine encounter with our conscience, which is the voice of God in our soul; (3) through mystical experiences, which are rare; (4) through common intuitive religious experiences such as cosmic gratitude or awe or wonder, which is a kind of embryonic worship; (5) through death and the fear of death—the fear that is awe and wonder, not the fear of evil and loss; (6) through encountering beauty and the longing (*Sehnsucht*) it sometimes inspires for something indefinable and transcendent; (7) through the history of God's interactions with the Jewish people; and above all (8) through Jesus Christ.

But how do we know God in the second sense, through rational philosophy?

Skeptics and agnostics say we cannot. How could the finite know the Infinite? The answer is simple. It is the distinction between essence and existence. We cannot know God's essence any more than our pets can know ours. But we can know his existence, as our pets know ours. There are many things and events in our lives that reveal his existence, as there are things in our pets' lives that reveal ours. And some of these can be put into logical arguments like the ones mentioned in chapter 33.

At the opposite extreme from agnostics, rationalists (like Spinoza and Hegel) say we can know God essentially and adequately. It is obvious to anyone who really does know God that these brilliant but arrogant philosophers simply do not know what they are talking about. They are dealing with concepts only, not with realities.

The right answer, as usual, lies between two equal and opposite errors. It is that we can know (*wissen*) three kinds of things about God:

1. We can know what God is *not*, and we can know this literally and univocally (using terms that have only one clear meaning). For example, God is not an animal or a mere concept or an impersonal force.

2. Using terms that are analogical rather than univocal, we can know what God is *like*, or rather what things are more like God than other things: God is more like the father of the prodigal son than like the elder brother; more like a good shepherd than a bad one; more like a shepherd than a sheep; more like a human person, who, being a person, bears his image, than a thing, which does not; more like sensory beauty than sensory ugliness; more like biological life than biological death; more like a sage than a fool; and above all more like a saint than a sinner.

3. We can also know how God is *related* to his creatures (both by transcendence and immanence or presence). We can know some of God's *actions* toward his

creatures: creating them, preserving them, loving them, manifesting himself to them through prophets, saints, miracles, and divine providence.

That imperfect knowledge is quite enough to make us responsible to God, as Saint Paul argues in Romans 1. We are responsible only if we are able to respond (response-able); and we are able to respond only if we are first addressed—that is, only if God first reveals himself to us; and as Saint Paul says, God has revealed himself to all rational human beings quite apart from religious faith in two ways: in nature and in conscience, in what Kant famously called "the starry sky above and the moral law within."

36

If There Is a God, Why Is There Evil?

The shortest answer to why there is evil if there is a God is not a sentence but a look: into the mirror.

But we also need a philosophical and theological answer.

The "problem of evil" is surely the strongest argument for atheism. Atheists argue that God and evil are logically incompatible; that at least one of the following four propositions must logically be false: (1) God is omnipotent, (2) God is omnibenevolent, (3) God is omniscient, and (4) evil exists. For if (1) God can eliminate all evil and (2) wants to and (3) knows how to, then evil would be totally eliminated. Since it is *not* eliminated, since there is both physical and moral evil, both pain and wickedness, there is therefore no Being who is omnipotent, omnibenevolent, and omniscient—no God.

Saint Thomas formulates the argument most simply: "If one of two contraries [opposites] be infinite, the other would be altogether destroyed. But the word 'God' means that He is infinite goodness. If, therefore, God existed, there would be no evil discoverable; but there is evil in the world. Therefore God does not exist."[1]

Aquinas' answer is not to deny anything in the premises but to add something to it: time and free will.

First, time: God does indeed eliminate all evil, but since his creation and his image in man are both in time, this

---

1   Saint Thomas Aquinas, *Summa Theologica* I, q. 2, a. 3, obj. 1.

elimination of both physical and moral evil, like the coming-to-be of both, is a process, like everything else in nature, and its fulfillment comes only at the end of the drama. So Aquinas replies, quoting Augustine, "Since God is the highest good, He would not allow any evil to exist in His works, unless His omnipotence and goodness were such as to bring good even out of evil."[2] The supreme example of this is the Crucifixion of Christ, the murder of God incarnate, which Christians celebrate as "Good" Friday, the salvation of the world. Out of the greatest of evils God brought the greatest of goods.

Second, free will. If man does not have free will, he is not a person, not a moral agent, and all moral language is meaningless. We do not command, counsel, reward, punish, or praise machines, no matter how complex they are. If man has free will, he can sin and do evil. Thus, the origin of moral evil is not God but man's free will (and that of the angels, some of whom chose to rebel and become devils).

Physical evil, on the other hand, is inherent in the nature of matter, for two bodies cannot occupy the same space at the same time, two plants cannot both receive the very same water droplets, and two animals cannot eat and nourish each other. The cosmos below man must run by the survival of the fittest. To live is to suffer, at least physically.

An omnipotent God could indeed have made matter totally subject to the human will, so that whatever we desire would happen by a kind of magic of mind over matter. But that would have made human community, communication, and relationship impossible, for it would mean each person living in his or her own self-created dream world. It would mean the truth of the philosophy of "create your own reality" or "you can be whatever you want to be," which is the lie sold by the devil to Adam and Eve in Eden.

---

2   Ibid., I, q. 2, a. 3 ad. 1.

Also, that "magic" would have eliminated physical evil (suffering) but not moral evil (sin). And once we fell into sin and selfishness, as we have in fact done, such a magical power over matter would be like putting nuclear bombs into the hands of two-year-olds. In fact, that is a good description of what modern man has actually done with his technological progress and moral regress. The most efficient possible formula for disaster and self-destruction is to maximize power (which we have done by radically increasing our technology) and minimize morality (which we have done by radically reducing our traditional morality and by treating freedom as an end rather than a means, as an intrinsic good, not subject to moral truth, restraint, and self-control, which is seen as oppressive).

Is it perhaps just barely possible that God is wiser than we are in doing the opposite, in limiting our power and enlarging our morality? That the key to human flourishing is not the elimination of suffering by power but the transformation of it by sanctity? That the practical answer to the problem of evil is not the submission of nature to man's "will to power" but the submission of man's will to God?

That surrender is the solution to the problem of evil, not just in theory but in practice.

37

What Is the Relation between God and Time?

Is God, like us, in time and change, in "process"? Process theology claims he is, because it claims that if he is not, then we cannot have personal relationships with him. How can we have a personal relationship with something that never changes, like an idea or a principle? Another argument for putting God in time is that God is a Person, or three Persons, and how can God be a person if he does not respond differently and changingly to our different and changing attitudes?

The answer is simple: the sun continues to shine in the same unchanging way whether or not its light is blocked by clouds or clothing or sunblock, but our relationship to it changes even though the sunlight does not change, because we do. Think of a pendulum, as on a grandfather clock. The ball is us in time; the hinge is God in unchanging eternity; the arm is the relationship between the two, which changes even though the hinge does not. God is love, infinite love, love that cannot be lessened or increased or changed; but that perfect and unchanging love is received and experienced in changing ways by changing human beings: as bliss when we are saintly, as the appeal to free will when we are choosing, as the offer of forgiveness and mercy after we sin, and as the threat of justice when we refuse to repent.

The God who is pure love can be experienced as a threat and an enemy. Remember that time when you were maybe five years old and in a really nasty fit of rebellion and wrath and your mother hugged you and kissed you and you felt tortured instead of comforted?

Most Jews and Muslims believe, as Christians do, in God the Father as someone who is eternally perfect and unchanging, and they do not believe, as Christians do, that God entered time in the Incarnation, in Christ. If, as process theology claims, it is impossible to have a living, personal relationship with a timeless God, then Jews and Muslims could not have a living, personal relationship with him—which they definitely seem to have, even though they do not believe in the Incarnation. The data of Jewish and Muslim holiness refutes the hypothesis that is the premise of process theology, that a personal religious relationship requires a changing God.

If God is perfect, God cannot change, for a change is either the addition or the subtraction of some perfection, so if God changes, he must lack some perfection either in his past or in his future.

Ascribing change to God's essential nature also seems to logically contradict the essential Christian dogma of the Incarnation of God *into* time. If God always has time and change, the idea of his stepping into time and change is like the idea of a fish stepping into the ocean.

The denial of God's eternity and timelessness also makes the reconciliation of free will and predestination impossible (see chapter 38), for eternity is one of the necessary assumptions of that reconciliation.

Process theology also seems to make the act of God's creation of the universe impossible, since time is relative to matter (Newton was wrong; there is no absolute time) and God is not material. If God created matter, he must have created time, thus he must transcend time.

This issue is, of course, a theological issue, but it is an issue of natural or rational or philosophical theology rather than of revealed theology. Solving it does not presuppose faith and divine revelation, but it simply logically critiques an idea—an idea that the orthodox faith of the three theistic Western religions also reveals the answer to. And it is the same answer, for revealed faith and right reason cannot contradict each other, since truth cannot contradict truth.

38

Can Free Will and Divine Predestination Be Reconciled?

A God with limited power is not worthy of the name "God." But a man without free will is not worthy of the name "man" either. Moral heroism, creative imagination, and intellectual wisdom cannot be expected from machines.

Divine sovereignty, omnipotence, omniscience, and predestination seem to contradict man's freedom. This was the idea that led both Sartre and Nietzsche to atheism. Sartre argued that if God existed, man was reduced to a machine, a product, an object, an effect rather than a cause. Nietzsche also, on a more gut level of will and feeling, confessed that he could not endure living in a world where there was a God who knew and mastered everything, including himself.

How can these two freedoms coexist—God's unlimited freedom and man's limited freedom? The answer is in an analogy: both exist in the same way as, from the point of view of Hamlet, Shakespeare's unlimited freedom and power and Hamlet's limited freedoms and powers coexist. (Freedom and power are not quite identical, but they imply each other: both are diminished by death, despair, disease, paralysis, prison, persecution, tyranny, and torture.) In fact, it is precisely Shakespeare's power to create anything he wills that is the source of Hamlet's free will, just as that same power is the source of the nonfree nature of Hamlet's sword and castle. God's power *created* our free will.

Every good story ever told by anyone (including God!) has these two dimensions that we could call predestination and free choice: the transcendent power and freedom of the author and the limited power and freedom of the characters. The characters must have free will because no one ever wrote a great drama about machines; and the author must have predestining power to give the story a destiny rather than mindless randomness. No story ever arranged itself and its own events and characters without the creative will of the author and storyteller. That is true both of man's invented fictions and God's created facts. Our creativity, unlike God's, is limited to fictions; even Shakespeare cannot make a real-world Hamlet, unless he procreates one—which is the most powerful and creative and godlike thing a human being can ever do, a far greater achievement than any mere artist's masterpieces.

To think that God cannot create genuinely free characters is to deny not only the characters' free will but also the divine Author's sovereign power. It is also to assume that God and his creatures are rivals that limit each other, like Shakespeare versus Ben Johnson as competing authors in Elizabethan England, or Hamlet versus Laertes as competing swordsmen in the castle at Elsinore. But that assumption is false, since grace perfects nature rather than diminishing it, as light perfects colors. Light transcends all colors; therefore it perfects all colors. And God transcends his creatures; therefore his grace perfects all creatures and their powers, including free will.

It is God's eternity that allows divine predestination and human free will to coexist. *Eternity* does not mean "ongoing time without either beginning or end" but transcendence of time itself. If God were in time, his omniscience would include foreknowing the future with certainty, and if God foreknew with certainty that you would be run over by a truck tomorrow, you could not choose to avoid that even if you never left your house. Perhaps the truck would demolish your house, or perhaps your house would be carried by a tornado into a stadium in the path of a speeding truck at a monster-truck rally. If God infallibly foreknew today that you would choose to murder your mother tomorrow, you could not choose to abstain from that act, any more than a robot could; and therefore you would not be free and responsible for it. But if God is *not* in time, he does not literally *fore*know anything, any more than he literally remembers anything; he simply knows everything. He, in his present, knows, in his present, everything, including that which is to us past or future. He does not push dominoes; the universe does that. He does not force us to act freely (that is a self-contradiction). He simply watches us make free choices, some of which are now past to us, some present, and others future. But they are not in his past or future because he has no past or future. To have a past and a future is to be limited by them, thus not to be infinite. His infinite being and knowing does not have the limitation of any dead past, any already-finished-and-determined past, nor does his being or knowing have any unborn and not-yet-real and not-yet-determined future. He is Life itself, not dead past or unborn future. In other words, there is no "*pre*-destination," just destination.

39

Can God Create Something Out of Nothing?

God cannot create something out of nothing if that is a self-contradictory and therefore meaningless concept, like omnipotence making a rock bigger than it can lift, or infinite goodness being evil, or God making the past, which has already been real, not to have been real. A self-contradictory and therefore meaningless set of sounds does not somehow suddenly acquire meaning when you add to it the words "God can do this."

But it is not self-contradictory for omnipotence to create, to make something out of nothing (*ex nihilo*). In fact it is not self-contradictory for God to make *everything* out of nothing, everything except himself (for something creating itself is indeed self-contradictory and impossible). And that includes everything in the universe of matter and also everything in the universe of spirit (angels). To create is possible for God because nothing limits and opposes and stands in the way of omnipotence. "With God all things are possible" (Mt 19:26). Self-contradictions are not things at all. They are not even thinkable.

Finite things have finite powers and can be defined. They can be *conceptually* limited because they are *ontologically* limited; we can define them because nature has already done that. (*Define* contains the same word root as *finite*.) Infinite Being has infinite power and cannot be limited either in fact or in thought, since thought mirrors fact.

We can define only what God is not, not what God is; and therefore God can be defined only negatively: for example, God is not an animal or an impersonal force or an abstract idea or a human being. In knowing what these things are, we know what God is not; and that is genuine knowledge, and very practical knowledge, because it avoids all forms of idolatry (confusing God with what is not God).

All gods that have ever been positively imagined or conceived by the mind of man have been idols because they could be defined and limited by human thought. And since they were limited in their being and in their being known, they were limited also in their power: they could not create something out of nothing; they could not be responsible for the very existence of the world. All the pagan philosophers agreed that the world (the universe) must be beginningless, not created but formed out of whatever stuff was eternal. They took for granted the universe's existence and asked only about its nature. Only after the God of the Jews had become known, largely through the triumph of Christianity, did any philosopher ever ask what Heidegger called "the fundamental question of metaphysics"—namely, "Why is there anything at all rather than nothing?" The new question arose in reason only after the answer to it had been revealed to faith. It was as if God set us a puzzle: "Here's the answer: because I created it. Now tell me, what's the question?"

When Philo of Judea went to Athens as the first Jew to study with the Greek philosophers there, they thought he was very wise when he spoke of a single God who was all-powerful, all-just, and all-wise. But when he added that this God had created everything that exists out of nothing, they changed their judgment and thought Philo had lost his mind. Not that the Greeks disbelieved in miracles or the supernatural, but there was literally in their language no word for the act of creation, as there was in Hebrew (*bara'*). That idea never occurred to any human mind or culture except to that of the Jews and those (mainly Christians and Muslims) who learned it from them.

The doctrine of creation has profound practical, existential consequences. If God is the cause of our very existence, we have no rights over against him, only over against each other. Our first reaction to that consequence may be that it sounds like God's reign over us is one of tyranny rather than justice, but it is the exact opposite: it is pure altruistic love, not justice, that must motivate all God's gifts to us, beginning with the gift of existence itself. For justice presupposes the prior existence of all the parties to it, but love does not. Justice is not creative, but love is. (Look at what happens in sex when we don't contracept it!) How could anyone who simply did not exist possibly justly deserve anything at all?

Another consequence of the idea that God is the Creator is this: if God is responsible for the existence of everything in the universe, it must all be ontologically good, even if some of it (like black holes and scorpions) is not convenient for us, and not all beings with free will choose to be *morally* good. Even the devil cannot abolish his ontological goodness, only his moral goodness. And that fact, his existential dependence on the God he hates, must contribute to his rage and his pain.

40

Does God Transcend Logic?

It is tempting for pious persons to think that God transcends logic, and to think that the more pious one is, the more one must deny any proposition beginning with "God cannot ..." Such piety seems to be not only a perfection of the moral will and heart and feelings, but also a matter of the perfection of the intellect and reason. After all, God the Creator transcends everything, including everything human. How could he not transcend our logic? Isn't our logic only human?

The only possible answer is, no, logic is not only human; it is divine. Logic is not "our" logic. We did not make it; that is why we cannot change it. We can change how it is expressed or formulated (we are its "formulators"; we formulate the propositions and write the textbooks, not God), but we cannot change its fundamental principles, as we can change the things that we invent. We cannot even *imagine* changing its fundamental principles: we can write fiction about universes in which there is no gravity, or in which time has a different nature, but not a universe in which 1 does not equal 1 but 2, in which the very essential nature of oneness and the very essential nature of twoness are not two different essential natures but only one.

Logic is not man-made, and therefore it is not relative to us. There is no such thing as American logic or Chinese logic, ancient logic or modern logic, feminine logic or masculine logic, liberal logic or conservative logic. There is just logic. Its fundamental principles are universal, necessary, and unchangeable.

The many principles of logic seem to be all based on one principle, expressed positively in the law of identity, that x=x, and negatively in the law of noncontradiction, that x is not non-x.

The reason why this principle, and whatever necessarily follows from it, is universally true and cannot even be conceived by the mind or imagined by the imagination to be untrue is because it is an expression of the eternal and unchangeable nature of God. God, the touchstone of reality, is identical with himself; that is why the logical law of identity is true. God does not contradict himself: that is why the law of non-contradiction is true. Logic is eternal; it is not a creature or a choice. "In the beginning was the Logic, and the Logic was with God and the Logic was God."

(Theologically, that quotation is potentially misleading because what Saint John was referring to as the Logos is a *Person*, the second Person of the Trinity, God's "Word" or "Mind" or "Ontological Truth," while logic is one aspect of the eternal *nature* of God that is common to all three Persons.)

Sophomore means "wise fool." It is a literally sophomoric question, and one that is often actually heard from sophomores, to ask, Can God make a rock bigger than he can lift? If so, there's something he cannot do: lift that rock. If not, there's also something he can't do: make that rock. Therefore the concept of omnipotence is self-contradictory. The answer is that the self-contradiction is not in the concept of omnipotence but in the concept of "a rock bigger than Omnipotence can lift."

Can the God who is unlimitedly wise not know anything? Can the God who is the source of all life die? Can the God who is infinitely good be even tempted by evil? The answer to all these questions is no, not by his divine nature, not unless

God adds a human, incarnate, temporal nature to his divine nature, which according to Christianity God the Son actually did. And thus it became true that God changed and grew from zygote to fetus to baby to teenager to adult, in every way that we do, including not knowing how to speak perfect Hebrew from birth. And it became true that God was tempted by evil, as the Gospels clearly affirm (his temptation was not a charade); and that God really died on the Cross (that was not a charade either). The second divine Person did all these things in his human nature, but not in his divine nature.

This problem may seem out of place for philosophy since it originates in theology, not philosophy; yet it is a philosophical problem, too, once it arises, and is subject to the laws of philosophical reasoning.

41

Is the Idea of the Trinity Self-Contradictory?

The idea of the Trinity certainly seems self-contradictory, for three is not one and one is not three, so God can no more be both one and three at the same time (or eternally) than he can be both green and not green, or eternal and not eternal. If, as the previous chapter argued, God does not transcend the law of noncontradiction, then God is not a Trinity, for the Trinity is a self-contradiction, it seems.

The reply is that the Trinity is not a self-contradiction because God is one in nature, essence, substance, or being, but three in persons. To have only one nature and to have three natures is indeed a contradiction, and so is being one person and three persons, but it is not a contradiction to be three persons in one nature, or one nature in three persons.

The same distinction (between person and nature) answers a similar question about Christ: it seems logically self-contradictory to say he is both human and divine, both Creator and creature, both eternal (out of time) and temporal (in time). But what is claimed by Christianity is that this one person has two opposite natures. Even we have something like two opposite natures, though not in the same way: we are both visible and invisible. Each of us is a single person, but each of us also has two opposite natures, or, more accurately, opposite properties of our single universal human nature, namely, both material and immaterial, both body and soul. (As we shall see in the next section, on anthropology, body and soul are not

two entities, like a ghost plus a machine; they are two properties of the same entity, like the meaning and the words of
a speech. You can't change either one without changing the
other—which is not true of ghosts and machines.)

The idea of the Trinity, the idea of God being both one
in nature and three in Persons, and the associated idea of the
Incarnation, of Christ as being two in natures (human and
divine) and one in Person, arises not from philosophical reasoning but from the biblical data: (1) God is one; there is only
one true God; (2) God the Father is God; (3) God the Son,
Jesus, is God (as he claims to be in many and varied ways);
(4) the Holy Spirit is God; and (5) the Father and the Son
and the Holy Spirit are not the same Person, but three distinct
Persons, for the Son obeys the Father and is sent by the Father,
as is the Holy Spirit. The only hypothesis that accounts for all
this data is the hypothesis of the Trinity.

There are no proofs of this dogma but also no disproof.
And there are also fitting reasons to believe it, for there are
clues, or analogies, of the Trinity in the universe. For instance,
space (height, width, and depth) and time (past, present,
and future) are both threefold; and the triangle is the first
among two-dimensional figures and the strongest architec-
tural structure.

There are also trinities in the soul, which is "the image of
God": in its three theological virtues of faith, hope, and charity; and in its three absolute values of truth, goodness, and
beauty. There is a trinity in Christ's self-identification as "the
way, and the truth, and the life" (Jn 14:6), which are parallel
to *sat*, *chit*, and *ananda* in Hinduism. There is also a trinity in
the soul's powers of knowing, willing, and feeling (or creativity), or mind, will, and heart, as perceived by psychologists
as diverse as Plato and Freud; and in the three dimensions of
every religion—creed, code and cult—in the three authorities
in Old Testament Israel—prophets, kings and priests—and

in the three corresponding protagonists in all our great epics (Gandalf, Aragorn, and Frodo; Ivan, Dmitri, and Alyosha Karamazov; Spock, Kirk, and McCoy in *Star Trek*; Hooper, Quint, and Brodie in *Jaws*; the lion, the tin man, and the scarecrow in *The Wizard of Oz*).

If God is only one and not three, God cannot be altruistic love itself (lover, love, and beloved) but only egotistic love, until he creates an other; but this would make God's essence and perfection, altruistic love, dependent on creatures, which is impossible.

Once again, as in the previous question, a problem that arises not in philosophical reason but in religious faith has great philosophical consequences.

42

Why Is Theism More Rational
than Pantheism or Deism?

Theism is certainly odder, trickier, more surprising, and less obvious to us than either pantheism or deism. A God who is "outside" the universe and a God who is "inside" it seem not only easier to imagine (since imagination uses spatial images) but also more logical, since God must be either identical with the universe (pantheism) or not (which seems to entail deism), either apart from the universe (deism) or not (which seems to entail pantheism). It's less easy to understand how any being can be both transcendent to and immanent in (or present in) any other being.

Two answers: (1) If God is a being like any other being, the theistic claim seems unreasonable. But theists do not believe that God is just one finite being among others, but that he is unique, the fullness of being. (2) If God created all other beings out of nothing, this allows him to be both transcendent to and immanent (present) in his creation, as an author is both transcendent to and immanent in the play or novel he creates.

Even within the universe, science is constantly reminding us that our expectations of the universe are too simple, and that the real universe, as revealed by deeper probes of science, is often much odder and more surprising and trickier than we expected. If even the creation surprises us, it would be most surprising if the Creator did not surprise us even more.

There are also insuperable problems inherent in both pantheism and deism.

Pantheism is essentially the identification of God and all things (*pan* means "all" and *theos* means "God"). For pantheism, the relation between God and the universe is like the relation of whole to part or soul to body: God is either the whole of which all things are parts, or modes, or appearances, or else God is the universal soul, or life, or meaning of all things, like the unity of a work of art. For pantheism God is not a Person with a personality and a character and a will and moral commandments, but an impersonal, all-inclusive Force or Consciousness. So the God of pantheism is not as great as the God of theism, just as *Hamlet* (the play as a whole) is not as great as Shakespeare, its transcendent creator. And if God is that "than which nothing greater can be conceived,"[1] reason is on the side of theism rather than pantheism.

Also, if, as pantheism claims, God is all things, then God must be evil as well as good. So pantheism does not have an absolute morality, since God is manifested in Hitler as well as in Jesus, in sin as well as in sanctity—which is indeed the God of George Lucas' pantheistic *Star Wars*, which is derived from nondualist Hinduism, in which Brahman, the supreme God, has a "dark side": he (or it) is equally Shiva the destroyer and Vishnu the creator (the maker). He (or it) has no personality, no character, no moral will, no commandments. Instead of giving us a moral law, he gives us diversity and inclusiveness training. He does not "discriminate." He is universally tolerant. He is the God made in the image of a nonjudgmental, super-progressive American pop psychologist. He is an equal, a chum. In fact, he resembles the chum in a chum bucket. He is all things to all men. He is The Blob.

If pantheists have a Blob God, deists have a Snob God, an absentee landlord, a deadbeat dad, transcendent but not immanent. But deism at least raises God above and beyond

---

1   Saint Anselm, *Proslogium*, ch. 3.

all creatures and allows us to adore and worship God but does not allow God to love and care about us. There is no room, in the infinite distance between the Creator and creatures, for personal intimacy.

Islam, though literally theistic, tends more toward deism than either Judaism or Christianity does, except among the Sufis. Judaism, though rejecting the Incarnation, nevertheless has always preserved a kind of intimacy with God, like Christian theism. It has preserved the paradox of transcendence and immanence.

The deistic Snob God is as imperfect as the pantheistic Blob God. It lacks something: full knowledge and love of everything that is not God himself. Aristotle, philosophy's greatest deist, argued that a perfect and eternal God would not know or care about temporal and inferior creatures because that would sully and demean his own divine perfection. Clearly the God of deism is another god made in the image of man and man's politics: not a democratic one, but a monarchical one.

Pantheism and deism are popular mainly among philosophers and theologians; theism (in its Jewish and Sufi as well as Christian varieties) has always been more fruitful and joyfully embraced by the masses of saints and hobbits and ordinary people.

Many Americans are both pantheists *and* deists, for on the one hand, they think of God as not superior, not hierarchical, not monarchical, but on the other hand, they think of God as "watching us from a distance," and think of heavenly union with God as "pie in the sky bye and bye." Errors often come in contradictory pairs: the bully is often also a coward, despair is a form of pride, and our modern individualism is both a collectivism and a conformism.

Part V

Philosophical Anthropology

"Know thyself" was the first commandment of the Delphic Oracle in ancient Greece. Socrates, the world's first and archetypal philosopher, interpreted this to mean not "Go see a shrink to discover all the ins and outs of your unique individual personality" but "Understand what it is to be a human being, discover the meaning of human life, know the essential human nature and purpose that you share with all other human beings."

But this command presupposes that there is such a thing as a universal human nature. In other words, it presupposes that metaphysical nominalism is false. Thus, one's (philosophical) anthropology depends on one's metaphysics. And both epistemology (the philosophy of knowing, of how human beings can know and do know and should know) and ethics (the philosophy of the human good or human rights or human duties) depend on anthropology. For as we have seen in our epistemology section, human knowing depends on human nature: if we are pure spirits, like angels, our knowledge is purely spiritual and intellectual; if we are purely material biological organisms, like animals, our knowledge is purely empirical and bodily; and if we are metaphysical amphibians, with a psychosomatic unity, our knowledge is like a two-bladed scissors. And as we shall see in our ethics section, the good for man obviously depends on the nature of man and is different from the good for either angels or animals.

But the question of the nature of man is meaningless for a nominalist. And so is the question of the distinction between man and other animals, for if there are no essences, there are no essential distinctions.

Thus, we have wild and mad philosophies of man that are much wilder and madder than any of the many philosophies of God. Some say that man is a god with amnesia. Some say that man is the inventor of illusions like mind or thought or spirit; the thinker that thinks up myths like the reality of thinkers and thinking. Some say man is an angel, a spirit, trapped in a body, a ghost trapped in a machine. Some say man is simply the cleverest animal, with a brain that is "a computer made of meat." Some say that man is simply a complex machine or a chemical equation. Some say that man is a devil, or the invention of the devil, doomed to pain and frustration. Some say man is a cosmic evolutionary accident. Some say that man is whatever he wants to be, dreams of being, or thinks he is. And some say that man is only a word invented by those who hate and fear women.

The central crisis of our contemporary Western culture, according to its greatest Christian critics like Pope Saint John Paul II, Pope Benedict XVI, and Aleksandr Solzhenitsyn, is its philosophical anthropology. And it is easy to see why. If man is in fact made in God's image, then once God is denied, forgotten, or reduced, the same thing happens inevitably to man, just as when a real thing is removed from in front of a mirror, its image in the mirror is also removed.

43

What Is the Soul?

The word *soul* means simply "life." The origin of the idea is not religious at all, but commonsense observation. Imagine a primitive man who owns two cows. One dies. Primitive Man is far from primitive in the keenness of his sense observation. (That is why he survived.) He observes that there is no difference in the bodies of the two cows. Dead Cow is udderly complete. But it cannot move its body and has stopped breathing. Primitive Man concludes that what is missing is breath or "the breath of life" or "soul." For what doth it profit a cow to gain the whole world but lose its own soul? But this reality, this "soul," is not made of matter. It is not a bodily organ, not even a brain. In other words, Primitive Man is not primitive enough to be a materialist and confuse invisible mind with visible brain. It takes super-sophisticated Modern Man to be that primitive. Only someone who thinks like a computer could reduce man, who invented and programs and uses computers, to a supercomputer, or could utter a self-contradiction like "artificial intelligence" or "intelligent machines."

If we dare to be as "primitive" as Aristotle, we also notice that there are three different kinds of souls. The souls of plants enable them merely to grow from within, as rocks and seas and sand do not do. The souls of animals enable them to move, to feel, to desire, and to sense the material world. And the souls of humans enable them to understand abstract ideas like the soul, to have self-consciousness and therefore distinctively human emotions like guilt and gratitude and greed, and to make free choices.

Our culture is materialistic in its practice, and this makes it materialistic in its thinking. Thus, when someone dies in the old movies, the old movie maker (who still believed there *was* a soul, as the new movie makers often do not) will usually show the soul rising above the body as a kind of thin gas, or ectoplasm, as if bodies are more solid and substantial than souls, and as if bodies contained souls rather than vice versa, as if bodies are like heavy suitcases and souls are like pretty flowers inside them. The image should be reversed: insofar as there is any physical image of a soul at all, it should be heavier, not lighter, than the body because it is more substantial and essential. It is the body that is thin and fragile and ephemeral.

Also, as Saint Thomas says, bodies do not contain souls, but souls contain bodies.[1] Bodies can only contain other bodies, but souls "contain" bodies as stories contain settings before settings contain stories. And life is a story, not a setting. Plays have settings only because they are plays, not vice versa. The physical setting is only one of the five aspects of the play, the others being the plot, the characters, the theme, and the style.

Aristotle and Aquinas say that the soul is the form of the body and, correlatively, that the body is the matter of the soul. They make up a single substance or entity or being, not two. The technical name for this is *hylomorphism*, or "the ism or theory of matter and form." Modern psychology calls it the "psychosomatic (body-soul) unity." We are neither ghosts nor machines, nor ghosts in machines. We are humans. We are little sacraments, little incarnations. We could call them incarnated spirits or spiritualized bodies.

---

1   Saint Thomas Aquinas, *Summa Theologica* I, q. 76, a. 3.

44

Which Is Prior, Intellect or Will?

The two distinctively human powers of the soul that other animals do not have (though some come closer than others to having them) are intellect and will, or reason and free choice. Animals have intelligence, but not abstract rational intelligence; and they can be willful, but their wills are not free to choose. They are like human infants, unable to rise to the understanding of universals, either theoretical or practical (moral). They are also full of healthy (and unhealthy) instincts but not yet capable of free and responsible choice and either sin or sanctity. To use an image from C. S. Lewis, their instincts are like the keys on a piano, but they have no sheet music to tell them which keys to play when. Their strongest instinct always wins. (This is not the case with us. We can fast.) We all know this; that is why we *train* them (both animals and infants who have not yet reached the age of reason) rather than *educating* them rationally.

Which of these two distinctively human powers, the abstract rational intellect or the moral will, is prior? This is really two questions in one: Which is prior in time, as the cause of the other, and which is prior in value?

We seem to have a dilemma. On the one hand, if we say the intellect is prior, we become rationalists, we seem to have to agree with Plato that all moral evil is caused by intellectual ignorance, and we seem to make the freedom of the will impossible, since the will is determined by the intellect.

On the other hand, if we say the will is prior, we become voluntarists and justify rationalization, as if the will had the authority to tell the intellect what to think.

Applied to God, intellectualism seems to make everything necessary, with no room for free love, and voluntarism seems to make everything ultimately arbitrary, with no absoluteness to truth. It is the problem of *Euthyphro*: is a thing good only because God wills it (*Euthyphro*'s voluntarism), or does God will it only because he knows that it is good (Socrates' intellectualism)?

The solution for God is easy: the two are identical. There is no gap in God, in time or in value or in causality, between mind and will, truth and goodness. God's knowledge of the good *is* his will to the good, and his will *is* his knowledge. There is a real distinction between the three Persons of the Trinity but none between any of the attributes of his single divine nature in themselves, only to our perspective. For all God's attributes are essential, not accidental, and his essence is one. Therefore, his justice *is* his mercy, and his mercy *is* his justice. And his wisdom *is* his love, and his love *is* his wisdom.

There is a real distinction in us, though. Our will can act contrary to our reason, and our reason can think contrary to our will. There are causal relationships between our two powers: one is before the other in causality, in time, and even perhaps in value.

But there is no single relationship and priority, as both intellectualism and voluntarism mistakenly claim, but a double and reciprocal one. It is like sexuality, a complementarity based on differences: men need women, and women need men. And so with us, will needs mind, and mind needs will. (And this is true also of value: men are superior to women at being men, and women are superior to men at being women.)

The double causality works because there are different kinds of causes. The mind is the formal cause of the will, the navigator who makes the maps and determines the right direction for the will to choose. But the will is the efficient cause of the mind, and commands the mind to think or not to think, with a will to truth or a lack of that will (or even, as Nietzsche demonically praised, a will to untruth). Each power determines the other in a different way, somewhat as men and women do, though that difference is not a difference between two of the four causes, as this one is. This solution comes from Aquinas.

Which is higher in value? Aquinas also says that the knowledge of things below us (the world) is higher than the will to it and the love of it, but the love of God is higher than the knowledge of God. That is because love conforms and transforms the lover into something more like the loved object, while knowledge subjects its object to the conditions and limitations of the knower. Thus, when we love God we become more godlike, and when we love the world, we become more world-like or worldly; but when we know God we can know him only in accordance with our minds' limitations, so that we drag him down to our level, so to speak; but when we know the world, we raise it up to the spiritual level of our minds, our souls. Loving God lets him divinize us, and knowing the world humanizes it.

45

Do We Have Free Will?

There is a dilemma regarding whether or not we have a free will, for if we do not, all moral language is meaningless, for we do not praise or blame or counsel or command or reward or punish machines for doing or not doing their work; and if there is no free will, we are only very complex machines, perfectly predictable in principle.

But if we are genuinely free, then our choices happen without any cause, and that is irrational and impossible, since nothing happens without a cause. Everything in time, everything that changes, everything that begins has a cause that explains why it begins. Nothing simply pops into existence without any reason at all. If that were so, we would find dragons, mountains, and palaces suddenly appearing in our front yards.

But if we are determined by prior causes, we are not free. Dominoes that fall because they are knocked down are not free to choose to fall or not to fall; and the universe seems to be a gigantic and complex set of dominoes, of which we are a part. But if, on the other hand, a domino freely chooses to fall, then it is not pushed and determined to fall by other dominoes. But we are in fact pushed, or caused, by all sorts of other forces, both within and without, both physical and spiritual, even when we make free choices.

William James tells the amusing parable of the philosopher in the street looking for a place to stay for the night and spotting two philosophy clubs, one on each side of the street: the Determinists' Club and the Free-Willers' Association.

He decides to apply to the Determinists' Club and knocks on the door. The doorman opens and demands to know why he came. "I came by my own free will," the philosopher replies, and the door is slammed in his face. So he crosses the street and knocks at the door of the Free-Willers' Association. The doorman opens and demands to know why he came. "Because they kicked me out across the street, so I had no choice in the matter." So that door is also slammed in his face.

The story is autobiographical, since James was an open-minded agnostic about most philosophical questions, including this one. So he simply decides, by a free choice, to believe in free choice, thus creating the answer to his question rather than discovering it.

We are indeed causally moved by many things, even when we make free choices; but not all causes are *determining* causes; they could be just *conditioning* causes—like advice, or temptations, or influences both from within and without, both spiritual and physical, from the soul or from the body. Our freedom is limited by these conditions, but not removed. When we are dealt lemons, not oranges, we are not free to make orange juice, but we are free to make lemonade—or not. Without many influencing and conditioning causes, we could not choose, so they are some of the *necessary* causes; but they are not *sufficient* causes, of our choice. They contribute, but they do not determine. *We* determine. We say, "*I* chose to do that because ..." And no matter what we add after the word *because*, the *I* is more than the *I*'s "becauses." We do not reward or punish becauses but persons.

The price we pay for denying free will is all moral meaning, language, and argument. The moral data—the experience of moral meaning, language, and argument—are concrete, massive, and tremendously important. They make an enormous difference. They are not questionable or iffy. It is the hypothesis of determinism that is iffy. The data should determine the hypothesis.

Yet here, too, we are free to choose despite the data. The choice not to believe in free choice exemplifies free choice just as much as the choice to believe in it.

Denial of free choice also makes love impossible. If we are not free, love is not free but determined by genetics, environment, evolution, brain wiring, and what we just ate for dinner. What an insult to humanity! We then have no right to say, "*I* love you," but only "My genetics, environment, evolution, brain wiring, and what I just ate for dinner loves you." Try that one on your Juliet, and you will see why women are better philosophers than men.

46

What Is the Role of Emotion?

One extreme, associated with Rousseau, claims that emotions are sacred and trump everything else in both power and value. Another extreme, associated with the Stoics, claims that emotions are at best distracting and tempting and need severe control by the reason, and that feelings of compassion and sympathy, far from being intrinsically good, as Rousseau says, are intrinsically unwise and harmful. It is obvious to the vast majority of ordinary people, however, that emotions, as distinct from reason and will, are neither intrinsically good or bad but raw material for the reason and will to inform well or badly, like horses that need to be tamed and ridden rather than either tied up or let run free at will. Thus, psychoanalysis, which deals primarily with emotions, when it is well done, can be an important aid to intellectual wisdom and moral virtue, as fertilizer aids plants or vitamins aid bodily health. To use Aristotelian language, a well-disposed matter more readily accepts right reason's imposition of form and order. This is true in farming, in art, and in morality.

It is obvious from experience that the two extremes of too much or too little attention to emotion can cause great troubles. Paradoxically, the Stoics, who tended to fear emotions and suppress them, really gave emotions too much credit and attention, by giving them too much fear. The other paradox is that the Rousseauian uncritical idealization of emotions and the refusal to educate and discipline them really neglects the emotions, just as the refusal to educate and discipline thinking neglects and devalues thinking.

Modern Americans almost always tend to classify love as an emotion, which makes nonsense of God's commandment to love, for emotions cannot be commanded. This is also a major cause of the breakdown of marriage, the single most important institution in human civilization, for it sees "falling in love" as the only reason for getting married and "falling out of love" as a reason for terminating a marriage, thus resting the skyscraper of marriage and the family on the shifting sands of always-changing feelings. Aquinas defines love as the will to the good of the other.[1] The better reason for marriage is to make the one you love happy, not to make yourself happy, because you have power over what you do to others but you do not have power over what they do to you. And—another paradox—seeking your own happiness usually makes you unhappy (as hypochondriacs, who worry about health, actually make themselves sick), while forgetting about yourself and your own happiness and seeking the happiness of the one you love makes you deeply happy.

The problem about emotions is murky partly because the word *heart*, in most European languages, is ambiguous: it could mean something deeper than emotions—the deep center of the self, the "I" that has or owns thoughts, choices, and emotions; or it could mean the source of all kinds of love, both emotional and volitional; or it could mean the will, as the master and captain of the soul; or it could mean simply the feelings, which is the usual popular meaning.

Those who make emotions central and intrinsically good are thinking of emotions like compassion, gratitude, wonder, appreciation, guilt, obligation, and awe—emotions (1) that are spiritual, not just biological; (2) that are "intentional"; that is, like thoughts and choices, about something

---

1　Saint Thomas Aquinas, *Summa Theologica* I-II, q. 26, a. 4.

other than themselves; (3) that even the higher animals do not have; (4) that involve something of free choice, since we can choose to accept and cultivate them or deny or ignore them; and (5) that are an essential part of morality, for we all instinctively judge persons without these emotions to be morally defective or incomplete persons.

On the other hand, those who see emotions as subhuman and distracting, if not positively a disvalue (like the Stoics), are thinking of emotions such as pleasure, pain, hunger, thirst, tiredness, contentment, sexual desires and satisfactions, loneliness, shame, and boredom, all of which are emotions (1) that are not spiritual—that is, from the distinctively human spiritual soul; (2) that are not "intentional"—that is, they are merely about themselves, not about any definable object; (3) that the higher animals also have; (4) that are purely passive and not freely chosen; and (5) that are morally neutral and mere raw material for the intellect and will to work on and use, to form and structure into good habits rather than bad ones.

Plato knew the importance of trained emotions (of both of the two kinds distinguished in the preceding paragraphs, the higher and the lower). That is why he mandated music and gymnastics (bodily exercise) as the beginning of early childhood education. For he knew that falling in love with beautiful forms in physical things like sounds and pictures and human bodies and their graceful actions is good training, at an age when rational and free choices are only embryonic, for the understanding and choice of morally good forms of action and life spiritually, which can develop more and more as the person matures.

In a culture that is half Rousseauian and half Stoic, and not clear about the status of emotions, Catholics need to be especially clear about this. This is true especially when it comes to sexual morality. We neither sanctify nor vilify passive emotions as such. On the one hand, we do not judge, as either virtues or sins, those passive and unfree emotions such as sexual desires, whether heterosexual or homosexual. Even when these desires are in themselves not rightly ordered but disordered, we are not responsible for the desires we inherit, only for the actions we choose.

Every religion in the world sees homosexual desires as objectively and in themselves intrinsically disordered. So are many heterosexual desires, but not because they are heterosexual. Every culture in history massively agreed with that judgment; ours has come to massively disagree with it. There has never been such a radical and massive moral turn in judgment in all of human history. That is a fact, not an opinion, and a good reason for thinking critically rather than passively about this issue, no matter who you are and most especially if you believe that sexuality was designed by God, not by man and media.

Emotions are neither virtues nor vices. "Falling in love" is not a moral virtue, and being tempted to lust (as distinct from choosing to give in to the temptation) is not a sin. What is subject to moral criteria because it is either virtuous or vicious is only our choice to embrace and encourage these passive emotions and to act on them when they are understood to be good or bad.

This explains why Catholics oppose hatred and discrimination against homosexual persons who are our brothers and sisters in our human family, yet also oppose homosexual sexual activities (and also many heterosexual ones).

This is probably the least understood and most passionately and widely opposed tenet of the entire Catholic faith today in Western culture—which says far more about that culture, which is addicted and obsessed with sex, than it says about our faith, which has many, many far greater things to say than this. And, of course, when the mother (or the Mother Church) gently and occasionally warns her teenager against his or her obsessive addictions, the teenager accuses the mother of obsessing about it. And when it is love that propels the mother to speak about it, the teenager calls it "hate speech."

47

What Is the Meaning and Importance of Sex, Marriage, and Family?

First of all, sex, marriage, and family have meanings. Sex is not just a biological and psychological fact; marriage is not just a cultural practice; and family is not just a social arrangement based on sex and marriage.

Secondly, because of these meanings, all three are much more important to human goodness, flourishing, and happiness both in this life and after death than our present culture admits.

As Pope Saint John Paul II has taught in his *Theology of the Body*, sex is a material icon of ultimate reality, the creative love that unites the Persons of the Holy Trinity. The meaning of anything is ultimately in its final cause (see chapter 25), its end, its purpose, its design, its perfection, what it is "for"; and the meaning of sex is first of all *persons*—both the creation of the children and the love and joy and unity of the parents.

It is also the supreme unification of both soul and body, and the total self-giving of both soul and body, including the body's fertility (except, of course, in rape, sodomy, or contracepted sex—by definition).

Our "throwaway society" (Pope Francis) and our "culture of death" (Pope Saint John Paul II) and our "dictatorship of relativism" about sexual morality (Pope Benedict XVI) denies or forgets the single most important meaning of sex: it is about babies. Procreation is the closest man can come to creation; the most godlike and creative thing human beings can ever do—namely, to produce the only things that have intrinsic and absolute value, the only things destined for eternal, infinite, unimaginable ecstasy, the only beings God loves for their own sake (and which we therefore must too). This forgetting of the very heart and essence of the meaning of sex is at the heart of all sexual sins, from fornication, adultery, and sodomy to contraception and abortion.

This is not just "Catholic morality" but (in varying degrees of clarity) the morality of all great premodern cultures in history. The "sexual revolution," which sees sex not as the reproductive system but as the entertainment system and sees children not as God's greatest blessings but as "accidents," is the most radical revolution in human history since the creation of the Church by the Incarnation of the Son and the Descent of the Holy Spirit. Nothing in history has ever succeeded in undermining and destroying religion in society more effectively: no polemics or persecutions, no plague or pestilence, no war or hatred, not even the most scandalous sins.

Sex is for marriage, and marriage is for family. Marriage is the first sacrament God instituted, in Eden. It is the most fundamental and total relationship between human beings possible in this life. It is the primary "horizontal" image of God's "vertical" relationship to us, a relationship of total love, fidelity, and self-gift.

The family, which is the designed product of sex and marriage, is not a merely biological entity, not a "litter," but is the single most crucial and fundamental institution in human life. All societies with stable families have thrived; all societies without them have decayed. The family is the only place where we learn life's most important lesson, self-forgetful love. Outside the family we are loved, if at all, only for what we can give (pleasure, assistance, service, convenience, entertainment, performance, utility, wealth, power) rather than simply for what we are (or rather for *who* we are).

Erase sex, marriage, and family from human nature and what is left? Not much more than either autonomous "angels" or animals with computers.

48

Is Mankind Good or Evil?

There are four possible answers to the question regarding if mankind is good or evil.

The answer of Machiavelli and Hobbes is that man is by nature evil—that is, selfish and competitive—and only force (Machiavelli) or fear (Hobbes) can change his behavior.

Marx is essentially a Machiavellian with an exit strategy. He believes that all history is the history of oppression; that man has been determined by society, society by politics, and politics by economics; and that with the triumph of Communism throughout the world by violent revolution, especially through the abolition of private property and religion, an eternal Utopia without oppression or conflict would ensue from pole to pole (such as now obtains in North Korea, Cuba, China, and some fashionable American philosophy departments).

The answer of Rousseau, sixties hippies, and pop psychology is that man is by nature good—that is, spontaneously compassionate, cooperative, and tolerant—and that it is social institutions and governments that corrupt him.

The answer of Aristotle is that man is born with neither innate goodness or evil but with potentialities for both good and evil, virtue and vice, and that his own choices, actions, and habits determine how much of each potentiality will be actualized. Although Aristotle believed that fate or chance determined much in life, to a large extent he also believed that "I am the master of my fate, I am the captain of my soul."[1]

---

1   William Ernest Henley, "Invictus."

Christianity believes that man is both innately good (because God created him in his own image) and innately evil (because he is born in Original Sin—that is, alienation from the active life and presence of God in his soul); and that as Thornton Wilder wrote, "There's a little good in the worst of us and a little bad in the best of us."[2] It also believes that we are destined, through suffering and through making and undoing many wrong turns, for eternal joy and perfection in heaven, in fact for a sharing in the very life of God; and also that some will freely refuse the grace of God that is our only hope of attaining this end. Thus, it is far more wildly optimistic *and* far more terrifyingly pessimistic, than any other philosophy about mankind.

Four data bases decide which of the four answers is true: a knowledge of history; an open-minded, unprejudiced observation of human behavior in both self and others; reading great literature; and common sense. All four of these data bases are declining in our current culture.

It follows that the securest way to answer the question is to restore the practice of exploring these four data bases.

The Christian answer is the most shocking and the most paradoxical—and the most interesting. Pascal's apologetic for Christianity is essentially to look at the data, which he summarizes as "man's greatness and wretchedness," which looks like a strangely shaped thing, like a lock in a door, and then to look at Christianity as an equally strangely shaped thing, like a key, and then compare them. Neither the lock nor the key seems reasonable at first, but they match. And the key opens the lock.

Freud uses a similar argument—the match between the human hand and the Christian glove—to argue for the opposite conclusion: that man created God in his own image and

---

2   Thornton Wilder, *Pullman Car Hiawatha*.

out of his own needs, especially the need for a father figure who could give him the superior wisdom and protection that his earthly father gave him when he was a child.

Atheistic existentialists argue that human evil refutes divine goodness. Christian apologists reply that the very judgment that so many things in human character and human life are indeed evil presupposes the knowledge of a standard of goodness that is absolute and divine. Only the height of the mountain can measure the depth of the valley. If the standard itself is only man-made and subjective, then so is the judgment and so is the "evil," so the premise of the atheist argument is invalidated.

A Greek agnostic argued, "If there is no God, why is there goodness? And if there is a God, why is there evil?" From the perspective of either atheism or theism, there are in the human data base strong evidence for the opposite position, and honesty must sympathize with the opposite position. Atheism is a faith, too, and it is a faith that is suggested, though not proved, by the human data.

Chesterton said that the strongest argument against Christianity is Christians. He would agree that that is also the strongest argument *for* it: saints. The best apologetic argument is to be one.

49

What Motivates Us to Be Wicked?

What motivates us to be wicked is much more difficult to answer than the previous one, even though it is less general and more focused. The motive for the evil we do is unclear and irrational because evil itself is dark and mysterious and irrational. In fact, our bad choices seem not only mysterious and irrational but literally insane at times; for we know by repeated experience that whenever we choose the morally good act—that is, an act that is just and loving, cooperative and altruistic—it makes us happy, deep down and in the long run; while whenever we choose the opposite, it makes us miserable, deep down and in the long run. Yet we often choose the misery rather than the joy. Why, in heaven's name?

Aristotle, our master of common sense, has a very helpful and accurate list of moral virtues and vices that is similar to that of Confucius; and he tells us what to do about the disease (namely, cultivate virtues by practicing the acts that lead to these good habits). But he does not tell us why we have the disease in the first place.

Socrates' answer, made famous by Plato, is that the origin of moral evil is moral ignorance—ignorance of the fact that what we all desire all the time (namely, happiness) can be attained only by justice, the virtue that includes all the other virtues. So the origin of our evil is our ignorant belief that we don't need virtue to be happy, that often injustice is more profitable (happifying) than justice. The fundamental point and conclusion of Plato's *Republic* is that that is illusory and false. So if we all read *Republic* and became totally convinced that it was right, we would all become saints, because we all seek happiness, and if we became convinced that only justice (virtue) was the way to happiness, we would all love and seek and practice justice as totally as we all love and seek happiness.

There are two problems with that answer. One is that we all know from experience that that conclusion does not follow, for many of us totally agree with the point of Plato's *Republic* but yet often choose the way to misery rather than the way to joy. The other problem is that Socrates does not tell us where we got that ridiculous belief that conflicts with all our long-range and deep-down experience, that belief that is so irrational. He sees the power of reason to move the will, but he does not see the power of the will to move the reason, to rationalize our stupid and self-destructive desires. On that point Freud the atheist and pessimist and moral relativist is wiser than Socrates the theist and optimist and moral absolutist.

The Bible's answer to our question is that we do evil first of all because we have the wrong *faith*: because, like Adam and Eve, we believe the devil's lies rather than God's truth. Our lack of virtue—especially the highest virtue of agape love, the third and highest of the three theological virtues—comes from our lack of the first theological virtue of faith and trust in God. The human plant is wrongly fruited because it is wrongly rooted (faith being the root and love the fruit). That lack of faith in God leads to our desire to grab the immediate joys that God is apparently denying us, the forbidden fruit. We see God as our rival rather than our loving Father; that's why we say "my will be done" instead of "thy will be done."

Christ's solution, which he both preaches and practices, even up to the Cross, is "thy will be done" rather than "my will be done"—not in the sense of a Stoical resignation but a total, childlike trust and love to God with our whole heart, soul, mind, and strength.

Buddha's answer to our question is similar to Jesus' answer negatively, but totally different positively. The negative part is that we experience the evil of suffering because we are selfish, that we have selfish desires or greed or grasping. And Christ would agree with that diagnosis, as far as it goes. But Buddha has no notion of sin, or of a God against whom we have sinned, or even of moral evil, because he does not believe in the soul or in free will. The only evil he deals with is suffering. And he says that the reason we suffer is because we have selfish desires, and we have selfish desires because we have the wrong belief: we believe we are real selves and that there are real goods that we lack. But he says that these are two false beliefs. The experience of enlightenment reveals that we are not ego-subjects that desire wrong objects; there are no real subjects or objects. It is not the ego that produces egotism; it is egotism that produces the illusion of the ego and its objects. Buddha denies both God and the soul, both the divine "I AM" and the human "I am," his image.

Hinduism's answer is that we do evil and experience evil because we do not experience the fullness of our own perfect divinity. Hinduism's supreme enlightenment is to tell us that "thou art that" (*tat tvam asi*): that what we really are is Brahman, eternal perfection, *sat* and *chit* and *ananda* (existence, consciousness, and bliss), infinite life and light and joy. We are God with amnesia.

Taoism's answer is that we are selfish and suffering because we do not follow the Tao, the way of nature that mirrors the way of ultimate reality that is beyond words but not beyond visible deeds—the deeds of spontaneous self-giving, like water.

Confucius, always the practical realist, does not have a theoretical account of the cause, only a practical account of the cure; and it is a map of the social and individual virtues necessary for maximum harmony and happiness. It is not an answer to our question (the diagnosis of the disease), nor is it a complete cure (he does not tell us *how* to move ourselves from vice to virtue), but it is a very useful map of the visible social dimensions of the cure.

The typically modern Western answer of our civilization—of Bacon, Descartes, and the so-called Enlightenment—is that we suffer because our conquest of nature by science and technology is not yet perfected. Once we have conquered human nature as we have conquered nature, Utopia will reign in a "brave new world."

In reaction to this optimism, the pessimistic answer of Machiavelli, Hobbes, Freud, Sartre, and many others is that there is no solution. Evil is just the way we are and the way things are, and there are only partial, temporary, and inadequate solutions.

For instance, for Machiavelli, it is the prince's personal conquest (*The Prince*).

For Hobbes, it is the law and order imposed by fear of the absolute monarch (*Leviathan*).

For Freud, it is the balance (homeostasis) or compromise between our id and our superego, between our true selves, which are our selfish, impersonal animal desires (the id) and our moral conscience, which is merely the reflections in our psyche of our social demands (the superego); and we achieve this partial peace by self-knowledge through psychoanalysis (*Civilization and Its Discontents*).

For Marx, we are miserable because of class conflict and oppression caused by the bad economics of private property, and the solution is Communism's classless society (*The Communist Manifesto*).

For Sartre, there is no answer, no peace in the hopeless war between our subjectivity ("being-for-itself") and objectivity ("being-in-itself"); no possible satisfaction to our impossible desire to be God, the synthesis of the two warring kinds of being (*Being and Nothingness* and *Existentialism and Humanism*).

For Nietzsche, we have been corrupted by both Socrates and Jesus (he would have added Buddha if he had known him). For Nietzsche, Socrates' "truth" is simply God without a face; and morality is the Jewish invention of the weak sheep to defang the powerful wolves; and Christianity is the master mistake, the synthesis of all errors. Nietzsche gave himself the same title as his book: *The Antichrist.* The solution is our will to murder God and to become the new god, the "over-man." It is "the triumph of the will," of the "will to power."

For Nazism, which is the politicization and racialization of Nietzsche's "will to power," what prevents this "triumph of the will" is the fact that the Aryan/German superrace has become polluted with inferior blood, especially that of the Jews (God's "chosen people"!), and the "final solution" is their elimination.

The progressive or "woke" Left of our time also focuses on race: that all our lives and education and politics are infected with the master sin of racism and its satellite sins such as the normativity of heterosexual marriages and families.

For deconstructionism, the problem is logocentrism, the belief in universal, absolute, and eternal truths, which must be deconstructed to reveal the hypocrisy of their concealment of their opposites. This is a tame, scholarly, intellectualized, and abstract version of Nietzsche's attack on both Socrates and Jesus.

50

What Is Happiness, and How Can We Achieve It?

Philosophers have given different answers to what happiness is and how it can be achieved, all of which are partially true and partially workable.

Aristotle noted that happiness (in the complete sense, not just subjective comfort and satisfaction, and not just objective perfection, but both together) is in fact the end that everyone desires in everything else and by means of everything else. No one seeks happiness for the sake of golf or gold or guns or girls or glory, but they seek all those other things because they think they will make them happy.

This is the question of the summum bonum or "greatest good," the final end or point or reason for all our striving and desiring and acting. Philosophers have identified this greatest good with duty (Kant), with moral virtue (Aristotle), with mystical enlightenment (Buddha), with knowledge (Plato), with power (Nietzsche), with pleasure (Mill), with fame and glory and honor and military success (Machiavelli), and even with sex (Freud). But none of these things, even when possessed, do in fact make us totally happy. Experience itself, not argument, refutes them all as inadequate.

Complete happiness would include both subjective (contentment) and objective (perfection) dimensions. If you feel like an angel, but you are really an ape, that is not real happiness, not complete happiness. And if you are really an angel, but you feel like an ape, that is not complete happiness either.

We possess neither complete subjective happiness (contentment) nor complete objective happiness (perfection), much less both together. Why?

Jesus goes to the root of the matter. The root of unhappiness is sin. So the root of happiness is sin's opposite.

Sin means, first of all, ontological separation from God; secondly, the consequent loss of moral goodness, love, and unselfishness in our souls and lives; and finally, consequent upon both, misery. Sinfulness, therefore selfishness, therefore suffering. Buddha, Plato, and Aristotle understood the evil of suffering and selfishness, but only Jesus understood the evil of sin.

Buddha's road to happiness is to stop desiring it. But we are incapable of doing that.

Socrates' road is the triumph of objective right reason over subjective selfish passion. We are also incapable of doing that.

Christ's answer is to heal the divorce between us and God. We are even more incapable of doing that. But he has done it for us, and our first task is not to do it but to receive it as gift, as grace, by faith. It is the only answer that actually works.

Nothing else does because we are inevitably and always unhappy, and our deepest hearts are restless until they rest in God,[1] our true "greatest good"—which can happen only by his grace and our acceptance of it by faith.

Once we do accept God's grace by faith, we see that our faith is itself also a grace, a gift. And that insight is still another grace. And in each of these acts of grace, God's grace does not substitute for our free consent but actualizes it. He does not turn our freedom off but on.

Obviously, philosophy alone cannot discover, decipher, or deliver this answer. Faith transcends and perfects all three acts of the reason: judging (discovering the truth), understanding

---

1   Saint Augustine, *Confessions*, bk. 1, ch. 1.

(deciphering the meaning), and proving (delivering the product). (See chapter 7.)

Philosophy alone cannot deliver this answer, but it can define and explore the other alternatives, which experience will show to be failures, thus hollowing out the human space for the divine answer, like a dentist who drills the rot out of the cavity before filling it. Augustine's *Confessions* is a classic example.

51

Is the Soul Immortal?

There are a variety of good reasons for believing that the soul is immortal.

The vast majority of people, cultures, and religions say it is. Some kind of God and some kind of immortality are pretty much a package deal that nearly all premodern sages teach. One must be something of a snob to say they are all seriously wrong about such a serious topic.

There is also Dostoyevsky's argument that there is no virtue if there is no immortality,[1] for if we never meet God and are judged by God after death, there is neither any final justice nor any final payoff for moral virtue. In that case, justice has nothing to do with reality; it is not done, only desired; it is merely our desperate subjective demand, not *real*.

There is also the argument from desire: since our desire for perfect happiness is universal, innate, and natural, and since perfect happiness cannot be obtained in this life, and since nature never plants in us desires for objects that do not exist, perfect happiness must exist in another life.

If souls die as bodies do, then the happiness we most deeply desire is simply unattainable, and nature is playing a trick on us in our very essential and inescapable being. If there is no immortality, life is a long abortion, and our hearts' deepest desire is thwarted. Life gives us many appealing appetizers, but then, once our appetites have been whetted, when the

---

1   Fyodor Dostoevsky, *The Brothers Karamazov*, pt. I, bk. 2, ch. 6.

main course comes to the table and the waiter lifts the cover and reveals it, it turns out to be nothingness. In that case, the source of the design of our lives is neither a wise and benevolent divine providence nor random chance but a malevolent and intelligent will that is telling a long and cruel joke.

Here is still another argument for immortality: If we are good and wise, we will love other persons as we love ourselves. And if we do that, if we truly love others, love will open our eyes and we will perceive that persons are indispensable and valuable in themselves, as ends, not merely as means, like tools and instruments to use. But if reality dispenses of persons at death as we dispose of dirty diapers, there is no basis in reality for this genuine love and respect for persons that is life's highest wisdom and life's highest value.

There are also theoretical arguments for immortality such as Augustine's argument that we can know with certainty eternal, absolute, unchangeable truths such as "2+3=5" or "justice is a virtue" or "eternal good is better than temporal good." It is not in our own or each other's changing minds or worlds that we see this truth. Our minds are in contact with an eternal mind. We already inhabit eternity mentally.

There is also Aquinas' argument that our souls perform two *acts* that the mortal body cannot perform, and therefore we are more than mortal bodies. The two acts are intellectual understanding of immaterial, abstract, universal truths and the will's choice of spiritual, immaterial, universal goods. Thus, we are more than bodies; and there is no need for spirits to die, as bodies do.

In fact, it is impossible for spirits to die, since (1) death is the separation of the parts of something made of matter, but (2) it is only matter that has parts outside of parts in space; souls, minds, or spirits have no separate parts, only separate powers and habits, all of which are the powers and habits of the same soul. You can't chop a soul up into parts.

If a thing dies, it dies either (1) by the simple annihilation of it as a whole or (2) by separating and dividing it into parts. But (1) nothing is simply annihilated; and (2) spirits or souls, unlike bodies, have no parts and therefore cannot be killed by separation into parts.

There is also Plato's argument in book 10 of *Republic*, that we observe many diseases can kill bodies, but the two diseases of the soul, ignorance and vice, do not kill souls, only wound them.

That's ten arguments for immortality. If even *one* of them works—any one—immortality is proved to be true.

52

What Happens at Death?

There are at least six different possible answers to the question regarding what happens at death.

The first is: nothing. Nothing that is us survives death, except the matter that once arranged itself into a human body and now rearranges itself into other things. In fact, some of the matter that is now in our bodies may once have been in another human body, as Hamlet explains to the king: the fish you eat may have been caught by hooking a fish with a worm that had eaten decayed flesh from a corpse. Some of your ancestors' atoms may be part of your body.

But if we are nothing but atoms, the "I" that these atoms presently makes up is not a person but a crowd of atoms. There is no "I." So how could a bunch of atoms make a mistake about a bunch of atoms? Even plants and animals are not just atoms, any more than a symphony is just notes or a book is just words. It's only what they are made of.

The second answer, pantheism, is the opposite negation of an "I." Materialism (the first answer) claims that everything, including ourselves, is only one thing—many atoms of matter—while pantheism claims that everything, including ourselves, is only one thing—a single all-encompassing divine spirit or mind. Materialism and pantheism are in one way total opposites, but in another way they are identical because they both deny personhood, selfhood, individual identity. They both make reality something like a tapioca pudding, for whether the pudding is material (answer no. 1) or spiritual (answer no. 2), we are all just lumps of the tapioca.

The third view, held by most pagan cultures, and perhaps even early Hebrew culture, is that the soul or spirit that survives death is a pale copy, image, or shade of the living self, a ghost that "lives" (if it can even be called life) in the deadlands, the darkness below, Hades or Sheol. When we die we do not become *more* real, solid, substantial, alive, happy, or in the light there than we are here, but less. In this way this third answer is closer to the nothingness that is the first answer (materialism) than pantheism is (the second answer), but it at least preserves some individual identity, as pantheism does not.

The fourth view, central to both Hinduism and Buddhism but also popular in ancient Western paganism, is reincarnation: that the same soul comes back in different bodies; that we are recycled. This is not wholly unreasonable because it appeals to our sense of incompleteness and imperfection: we sense that not only many of our ideas, but our very selves, are only "half baked" when we die.

The problem with reincarnation is not so much with the soul (it grants the soul immortality) as with the body, which it reduces to something wholly accidental to our identity, so that dying is only like changing motel rooms.

It also reduces the importance of life to one of many attempts to pass a test that no one can fail in the end, and thus the drama of life is gone. Life is not even a game because it is not possible to lose it. But if we live only once, we are motivated to live it well, with gusto and passion. If, as Scripture says, "It is appointed for men to die once, and after that comes judgment" (Heb 9:27), life is a great drama.

And purgatory does more justice to our sense of incompleteness and our need to finish the process of spiritual "baking" than reincarnation does, which can only imagine the "baking" to reoccur in the same old earthly ovens (i.e., mortal bodies and material worlds).

Reincarnation also assumes a two-substance theory of the self, and so does a fifth view, dualism, which claims that our souls survive and go to heaven (or hell) while our bodies simply decay and disappear.

But this view of the afterlife treats us like angels temporarily imprisoned in bodies. It does not satisfy our demand to be more, not less, complete persons after death. We *want* healthy bodies and resist losing them by death, disease, weakness, or pain. Our bodies are part of our identity. We do not "have" bodies as we have clothing; we *are* bodies as well as souls. We can't take our bodies off as we can take our clothes off. This dualistic view is too one-sidedly "spiritual": it reduces us to something incompletely human after death. We become something like plays that are only in the playwright's mind but not performed on stage anymore, like a computer program that is never used or sheet music that is not played.

This "spiritual" view also does not account for our present experience of the psychosomatic unity as does Aristotelian hylomorphism. It reduces our bodies to motel rooms that the real "we" moves out of, or to cars that "we" ride in. But we do not experience ourselves as pure spirits and our bodies as impersonal vehicles, mere material objects, unless we have a very serious psychological disorder. (An entire culture may experience very serious psychological disorders. The state of Original Sin is a very serious psychological disorder, although it is also more than that.)

The two-substance view is inherently incoherent. If we are spirits *plus* bodies, we are like ghosts living in machines. How could a ghost, that has no hands, push the buttons of a machine? Or how could a machine, which has no mind, understand matter as its object? Even the most complex supercomputers do not understand, choose, or feel anything at all, any more than the most complex libraries do.

The sixth view, the Christian one (and also the Muslim and Orthodox Jewish one), is distinctive in three ways in addition to the resurrection of the body and the Last Judgment.

First, it does not limit the afterlife to our imagination or conception. It affirms that "no eye has seen, nor ear heard, nor the heart of man conceived, what God has prepared for those who love him" (1 Cor 2:9).

Second, also implicit in the above quotation, it treats the afterlife as a personal divine gift of grace, not a state predictable or comprehensible from human nature alone by natural reason alone. In fact, in both the Western Catholic and Eastern Orthodox traditions, the afterlife consists in *theosis*, divinization, actually sharing in divine life, not by nature (as in pantheism) but by divine grace (2 Pet 1:4).

Third, since it is by the free choice of divine grace, this view therefore factors in the free choice of humans to accept it (for a gift must be freely received as well as freely given), and therefore the possibility of hell as well as heaven. If heaven is a divine gift, it can be refused, whether out of pride or despair or any other reason. Receiving it must mean (a) believing it with the mind, (b) freely accepting it with the will, and (c) loving it with the heart.

Part VI

General Ethics

53

Does Ethics Depend on Religion?
On Metaphysics? On a Philosophy of Man?

Obviously, religious faith is a powerful motivator for ethical behavior. But the knowledge of ethics or morality or right and wrong, does not depend on religion, religious faith, or supernatural divine revelation. God made man with a moral conscience, and that has only been wounded and weakened but not destroyed by the Fall.

Conscience is not merely a feeling (although it is that, too, especially the feeling of being obligated or duty bound) but first of all a knowing, an understanding: that there is good and there is evil, and that we are obligated to be good and to do good and not evil. And we all know what moral goodness means. The different religions and cultures of the world differ radically in their theology but not much in their morality.

However, although one's ethical philosophy does not depend on one's religion, it does depend on one's philosophical anthropology. For ethics is about what is morally good *for human beings*, and that depends on what human beings are, on what human nature is. If we think of ourselves as apes with big brains, our ethics will reflect that. If we think of ourselves as pure spirits trapped in bodies, our ethics will reflect that.

Philosophical anthropology, in turn, depends on metaphysics. Metaphysical materialism necessitates anthropological materialism, for if *being* excludes spirit, *human* being must do the same, and if human *being* excludes spirit, human *ethics* must too. Metaphysical immaterialism also necessitates anthropological and ethical immaterialism; and the same is true of two-substance dualism and of hylomorphism (matter-form unity).

When we think of ethics, we usually think first of all of moral laws or rules or commandments, and of moral virtues and vices as habits of obeying and disobeying those rules. It is true that a morality without rules is hardly conceivable, but there are also other and deeper dimensions of morality than rules.

And when we think of moral rules we usually think first of all of rules for treating each other. It's also true that a morality that ignores this is hardly conceivable, but there are other and deeper dimensions of morality than social rules.

C. S. Lewis gives us an unforgettable image for the three parts of morality.[1] Think of a fleet of ships. Their sailing orders, or rules for behavior, must tell them three things. First, how the fleet is to stay together and cooperate and not crash into each other or get in each other's way. Second, how each individual ship must stay afloat and shipshape. Individual ships without good captains or navigators will be harmful rather than helpful to the other ships and to the fleet. Third, and most important of all, what is the mission of the fleet? Are they to fight a naval battle, bombard a shoreline, ferry passengers, or carry freight, or is it a pleasure cruise?

We could call these three questions the three dimensions of ethics. They are separable in thought, but not in reality, like the three dimensions of space.

The first dimension symbolizes social ethics: how to treat each other. The second symbolizes individual ethics: moral character, virtues and vices. If you're not a good person, you won't do many good things to others. The third is the most

---

1   C. S. Lewis, *Mere Christianity.* "The Three Parts of Morality" is the first section of book 3.

important of all; it's about life's meaning and purpose and end, to which all the other goods are means.

The first dimension is about our relationship to others; the second is about our relationship to ourselves and our conscience; and the third is about our relationship to God, or ultimate reality. As Thomas Merton wrote, "We are not at peace with others because we are not at peace with ourselves, and we are not at peace with ourselves because we are not at peace with God."

Yet this most important question is the one most ignored or neglected or denied by typically modern people, who concentrate almost exclusively on the most derivative and dependent of the three questions, social ethics. But you can't have a good society without good members. A society of good individuals, even if it has bad institutions and laws and politics, will find its way to improve those institutions and laws and politics, while a society of evil people, even if it has good institutions and laws and politics, will find its way to corrupt those institutions and laws and politics. Social ethics is essential, but it is dependent on the other two dimensions of ethics, which go deeper. How people behave to each other publicly is observable to the senses, but an individual's moral character is, in itself, invisible; and the meaning of life (the mission of this fleet and each of its ships) is also not visible on any maps or list of laws and institutions.

The obvious reason modern thinkers reverse the hierarchy of importance among these three dimensions of morality is that it is religion that claims to answer the third and most important question, and the modern mind is defined by its increasing fear, indifference, or hostility toward religion. This is the obvious main theme of the story of Western civilization for the last five hundred years.

There is no contradiction between the first point made in this chapter, that moral knowledge does not depend on religious faith, and the last point, that religion claims to give an answer to the most important ethical questions. Similarly, there is no contradiction between the fact that the wrongness of slavery, abortion, and adultery is evident to natural reason and does not depend on religious faith and the fact that religion reinforces this teaching in declaring these things wrong.

54

What Are the Most Important
Moral Virtues?

Virtues are simply good habits; vices are bad habits. Habits are ways of acting that we cultivate by repetition. They reveal our character or moral personality. Moral character is the sum total of moral habits. The essence of what the previous chapter called the second dimension of ethics is the moral virtues.

Moral virtues are not the only kind of virtues. There are also intellectual virtues, such as good memory, logical order, and instinctively wise judgment. And there are artistic virtues such as creativity and technique. And there are also practical, technological virtues like competence and efficiency. There are also some virtues, such as patience and wisdom, that fit into more than one of these categories.

The tradition of identifying the four cardinal virtues of prudence (or practical wisdom), courage (or fortitude), moderation (or self-control), and justice (or fairness) is widespread, and it comes from many sources (e.g., Plato, Aristotle, and the later Wisdom literature of the Old Testament). They are called *cardinal* from the Latin word for "hinge": all other virtues hinge on them, turn on them, depend on them. They are necessary, though not sufficient, for good moral character.

Justice means equity but not necessarily equality. It means giving what is due or deserved: A's to A students, C's to C students; treating things of equal value equally and things of unequal value unequally. It is the three-Rs principle of right response to reality. Subhuman things should be used as merely things, not loved as persons or worshipped as God; people should be loved and respected, neither used nor worshipped; and God should be worshipped, not treated as an equal or used as a servant.

Religion adds the three theological virtues of faith, hope, and charity (active unselfish love). They are called *theological* because they are both directed toward God (*theos*) and are gifts of God and his grace.

Faith is more than belief or opinion; it is personal trust. Its ultimate object is God, and its immediate object is all the truths revealed by God.

Hope is more than the feeling of optimism; it is faith directed to the future and to God's promises.

Charity is also more than a feeling; it is to will the good of the other.[1]

There are always two opposite vices to every virtue. For instance, courage is the alternative to both foolhardiness and cowardice; charity is the alternative to both idolatry and indifference; hope is the alternative to both despair and presumption; faith is the alternative to both naivete and cynicism; and humility is the alternative to both pride and self-loathing.

All virtues are cultivated as habits by repeated practice, and practiced as deeds that actualize these habits through concrete choices that are made by the will, not just the mind or the emotions, although these other two powers are also involved, and either help or hinder.

A virtue that is presupposed by all other virtues is honesty, or the will to truth. It is directed not only toward others (telling the truth) but also toward oneself (both telling oneself the truth and listening to it) and toward God (both telling it to him and listening to it from him). It both seeks and tells and

---

1   Saint Thomas Aquinas, *Summa Theologica* I-II, q. 26, a. 4.

values truth everywhere. Truth is like light. If the lights are not on, the greatest artist cannot paint the easiest picture and the greatest surgeon cannot perform the easiest operation.

Other important moral virtues, recognized by nearly all cultures, are gratitude, forgiveness, humility, empathy, fidelity, kindness, respect (or reverence), and mercy. These all have an emotional dimension but their essence is volitional: we can will them or nill them.

These virtues are habits, not acts. They are all good in themselves, but they are not the whole of morality; they need to be actively applied in different ways to different circumstances. That is the role of prudence or practical wisdom. For instance, honesty is a crucial virtue, but it does not demand that Romeo answer yes to Juliet when she asks him, "Am I too fat?" or that the Dutch tell the Nazis the truth about where they are hiding the Jews. A "head fake" in basketball or boxing is not a lie. Justice and mercy are always demanded of us, but justice does not demand that the teacher always say no to a student's request for a second chance on a final exam that he flunked, nor does mercy demand that the teacher always say yes.

55

Is Morality Objective and Discovered, or Subjective and Invented?

The question regarding if morality is objective and discovered, or subjective and invented, is the question that most importantly distinguishes our typically modern Western culture from all the cultures in the history of the world. They all have some version of the natural moral law—for instance, the Greek Logos, the Chinese Tao, and the Hindu rita—an objectively real moral order or moral values or moral truth.

This notion—the idea of an objectively real, absolutely binding, and universally known natural law about what we ought to be and ought to do—is called the natural law (or the natural moral law to distinguish it from natural physical laws like gravity or relativity). It is called *natural* for two reasons. First, it is known by nature, by immediate moral intuition, by conscience, which is a *knowing*, not a feeling, although it is intuitive rather than calculative. Conscience needs to be developed and informed and matured, but it is as innate as our capacity for speech. Second, it is called the natural law because although it does not tell us, as physical laws tell us, what nature does in fact do but what we ought to do, yet it is based on human nature, on the objective facts and real needs of human nature. Murder is wrong because we need life; lying is wrong because we need truth; robbery is wrong because we need property.

For the first time in human history, the belief in the natural law is denied by the majority of "intellectuals" in our culture today, and therefore also, increasingly, for those whom they teach, either formally or informally. The modern position is called moral subjectivism (because it denies the law's objective reality) or moral relativism (because it denies that morality is absolutely obligatory) or moral skepticism (because it denies that this law is certainly known by conscience). The modern position claims that moral laws are human inventions that are "posited" by our will (thus it is called moral positivism) rather than discovered by our moral intellect or conscience; that morality is like art rather than like science, like a game or a machine that we invent rather than a truth that we discover.

The most usual argument for the modern position is that individuals and societies differ about moral laws and argue endlessly about them. Morality is not like mathematics; we all know and agree that 2+2=4, but we do not agree that capital punishment or abortion or sex outside of marriage is evil or that it is good.

But this very fact of moral argument proves exactly the opposite of moral subjectivism, for we do not argue about our subjective emotions or fantasies or dreams. If I say I feel sick, you do not argue with me and say I feel well. We argue about what is really true, not about how we personally feel.

And the premise of this argument of the relativist—that different individuals and different societies have different moral values—is simply untrue. Different individuals and different societies do indeed differ about concrete applications of general moral principles, but not about the fundamental principles themselves. In fact, behind every disagreement about how to apply a moral principle there must always be an agreement about the principle. And even disagreements about a *principle* always presupposes agreement about a more fundamental principle. For instance, those who oppose and those who favor capital punishment both agree with the principle that human life is a great good. Even radicals like Nietzsche who want to go "beyond good and evil" urge us that it is *better* to do that than not to, thus presupposing the standard of goodness itself; they only disagree about its particular content.

This agreement goes beyond the most general principle of "Do good, not evil." It goes into details of what moral good and evil mean. There has never been a society that values self-ishness, dishonesty, injustice, cruelty, folly, murder, theft, adultery, and selfishness as *good* and teaches that we should feel guilty about unselfishness, honesty, justice, kindness, wisdom, and respect for life, property, and sex as evils. The dis-agreements are only about either how to apply these principles or about which ones to emphasize the most.

We discover the origin and attraction of moral subjectiv-ism when we want to do something the moral law forbids (e.g., stealing, lying, committing adultery, disrespecting, kill-ing); but when the same things are done to us, we do not merely fight, like animals, but also argue, complaining that these things are unfair and unjust. We might rationalize and try to justify our own theft of someone else's place in a waiting line; but when our own place is stolen, we behave as though we believed in a universal, objective morality, and as if we expected the other person to know about it and obey it.

Spiritual roads, and their destinations, are just as true or false as physical roads. In the physical world, opposite roads do not lead to the same destination. You can't get to the Pacific from Chicago by walking east no matter how sincerely you believe you can and no matter how hard or how sincerely you try. In the world of logical thinking, opposite premises do not yield the same conclusion. In the world of mathematics, different solutions to an equation are not equally true. And we experience the same thing in the world of morality: different soul-roads lead to different soul-destinations. Moral goodness leads to happiness and an untroubled conscience; moral evil leads to unhappiness, at least deep down and in the long run, and a sense of guilt, whether that sense is repressed or not. A thing must first exist in the soul before it can be repressed.

The traditional notion of an objective, absolute, and universal morality is not merely a theory, a philosophy. We actually *experience* moral obligation, moral duty. We can suppress this experience, but not totally, and it is always there to suppress. (Read Dostoyevsky's *Crime and Punishment*!) We bump up against moral laws with our conscience just as we bump up against physical laws with our body and logical laws with our mind. We cannot make a circle that has corners, or an odd number by adding only even numbers, no matter how much we try. There is something other than the physical world that pushes back against us. Truth and goodness are no more our invention than the matter of the universe is. Alternative theories about the origin of morality may be clever and convincing when we think about them, but the data of experience must be the test of all theories and hypotheses.

56

Are There Inherent and Inalienable Rights?

Moral rights and moral duties are correlative. I am duty bound to respect your rights, and you are duty bound to respect mine. If there are no rights, there are no duties, and if there are no duties, there are no rights.

Rights are liberties; duties are responsibilities. Viktor Frankl, the Auschwitz survivor and author of *Man's Search for Meaning*, said that the Statue of Liberty in New York ought to be balanced by a Statue of Responsibility in San Francisco.

If rights are assigned by the will, they are revocable by the will. For instance, a traitor's right to vote or a drunk's right to drive. But if some rights are inherent in the very essence of humanness or personhood, they are irrevocable and inalienable. Whatever rights the state gives us, the state can remove; but since the state did not give us our inalienable and inherent rights, the state cannot remove them. Our Declaration of Independence begins with the assertion that "all men are created equal" and possess equal inalienable rights because these rights are given not by the state but by "nature and nature's God."

The objectively real causal connection between "nature and nature's God" (the cause) and natural rights (the effect) is not the same as the causal connection between *our subjective knowledge* of these two things. Our knowledge of the real effect can cause our knowledge of the real cause, as our knowledge of a fingerprint can cause our knowledge of the criminal who left it; but that psychological causality does not always work, as the objectively real causality does. We can know the effect without knowing the cause. We can also know the cause without knowing the effect. In other words, natural rights and God necessarily imply each other ontologically but not psychologically.

But the psychological causality often *does* work. We can argue from the top down, so to speak, from cause to effect, by arguing for natural rights from the premise of God as our Creator and Designer; and we can also argue from the bottom up, so to speak, from effect back to cause, and argue for the existence of God the moral lawgiver from the existence of the moral law and its natural rights that he gives.

But these two arguments are not equally strong psychologically. If you believe in God, you will almost certainly believe in natural rights, unless your God is amoral. But it is not equally true that if you believe in natural rights you will certainly believe in God. Similarly, if you believe in God, you will believe in objective truth and the objectivity of science, but one can believe in objective truth and science without believing in God. Thus, a belief in natural law and natural rights can be either sacred (with God) or secular (without God), since atheists and agnostics have reason and conscience too.

That is why appeal to natural law and natural rights can be universal, and not dependent on religion, as it was until recently. For all humans have natural reason, even though not all humans have supernatural faith. That is why the crisis of natural reason and natural law is even more fundamental and catastrophic for civil society today than the crisis of religious faith, and why an atheist who is a moral absolutist is closer to a Catholic moral absolutist than to an atheist relativist. Camus is closer to Mother Teresa than to Sartre.

Our Declaration of Independence declares not only the existence of natural rights, but its original version also listed three primary examples of it when it went on to say that "among these rights are life, liberty, and property." "Property" was changed to "the pursuit of happiness." We have no "right to happiness" (see C. S. Lewis' article with that title), but we do have a right to pursue it by morally licit means.

Life, liberty, and property are three natural rights that are in a certain order: possessing property depends on liberty, on not *being* another person's property; and liberty depends on life, since the dead do not have it. America fought the Civil War about the second right, liberty: Is it a natural, inalienable, universal right, or does it hold only for Whites? The West fought the Cold War about Communism and its denial of the right of private property, the third right. America is now fighting a war about the most fundamental right of all, the right to life: Does it apply to *all* human beings or only those lucky enough to have survived the most lethal place on earth today, a mother's womb?

It is not a religious belief but a scientific fact that human beings do not suddenly begin to exist when the two blades of the obstetrician's scissors cut the umbilical cord, but earlier, when a biologically and genetically distinct new individual comes into existence at conception. From this fact it logically and necessarily follows that abortion is in fact murder (deliberately killing an innocent human being), no matter what other surrounding feelings and factors are considered and no matter how serious they are. If all (innocent, nonlife-threatening) human beings have a right to life, it logically follows that unborn human beings do also. Whatever else is to be said about this issue by addition, that fact cannot be honestly or reasonably subtracted from it.

It is sometimes very inconvenient to respect others' rights; in fact it sometimes demands heroic sacrifices. But rights impose duties; and duties, unlike ideals or values, are not optional even when they require sacrifice. We are not duty bound to perform heroic actions that go beyond the call of duty. We are only *invited* to that. But we are *required* to perform our duties, and these include respecting others' inherent rights, beginning with the right to life, which is the presupposition and foundation for all other rights. Deny that, and the whole of morality can come tumbling down. Once that happens, to an individual or a culture, all of life unravels.

On this, as on all moral issues, especially very controversial hot-button issues, it is very important to distinguish the question of objective truth, the question of the objective rightness or wrongness of the act, from the question of the degree of subjective guilt and responsibility of the actor. The first is a black-or-white, either-or, zero-sum question; the second is not. And in practice, forgetting this second thing almost infallibly guarantees failure to convince "the other side" of the first thing. We must always be "speaking the truth in love" (Eph 4:15). Truth and love are our two absolutes because they are what God is. The marriage of truth and love in our witness is very fertile; their divorce is always sterile. Love without truth is a fantasy; truth without love is an enemy.

57

Is Each Person an Intrinsic End?

Ethics is most fundamentally about good and evil. Good is of two kinds: means and ends. Means are good for something else; ends are good in themselves. For instance, happiness is an end while baseball is a means to that end, since it makes many people happy. Some goods are both means and ends—for example, health, which is the end or purpose of medicine and surgery and also a means to many further ends such as sports and work.

Goods are also divided into ontological goods and moral goods. Ontological goods are "isses," moral goods are "oughts." All beings are ontologically good, but only some human acts are morally good. Even moral evils depend on ontological goods. It takes an ontologically good stroke of the axe to perform the morally evil deed of decapitating an innocent person.

Both ontological and moral goods are divided into means and ends. All ontologically good things are rightly used as means to the end of persons and their perfection, both physical (health) and emotional (happiness) and moral (holiness). That is why we should not love things as ends and persons as means but things as means and persons as ends.

Kant famously formulated this "personalist" principle— that all persons (i.e., rational beings, beings with reason and free will) are ends and therefore should be treated as ends, with respect, rather than merely used as means to other ends.

This was his second formulation of what he called the single most fundamental moral law or "categorical imperative"; and he deduced it from the premise of his first formulation of it—namely, to act always according to the maxim (practical principle) that you will all others also to obey. Jesus' version, often called the Golden Rule, is "Whatever you wish that men would do to you, do so to them" (Mt 7:12). In other words, love your neighbor as you love yourself. Confucius' version of this principle, often called the Silver Rule, is "Do not do to others what you do not want them to do to you."

The personalist principle logically follows from the Golden Rule because we all want to be treated as ends, as valuable in ourselves, and not merely to be used as means to other ends. And this depends on metaphysics (on what *is*) and on anthropology (on what *we* are) because the reason we should *treat* persons as intrinsically valuable ends is that that is what they in fact *are* in their being, their essence, their nature. Thus, both principles depend on the three-Rs principle: right response to reality. Even Kant, who was skeptical of traditional metaphysics, based his personalist principle about what we ought to do to persons on a metaphysical premise about what persons in fact are.

All moral evils violate this principle. This principle thus identifies all moral evils, but not all moral goods, for some moral goods are goods for, or duties toward, only some persons, not others (e.g., the duties of soldiers versus civilians, the married versus the unmarried, adults versus young children, priests versus laity, the sick versus the well).

58

Does the End Justify the Means?
(Utilitarianism)

Utilitarianism, which according to polls is the most popular moral theory in America, answers yes to the question regarding if the end justifies the means, while traditional natural law morality answers no.

Pragmatism is often confused with utilitarianism, but pragmatism is an epistemology, while utilitarianism is an ethics. Pragmatism is a method of thinking scientifically about practical problems, translating questions of theory into questions of practice—for example, asking about an idea, What difference to one's life would believing it or acting on it make? It identifies the *truth* (or more properly the meaning) of an idea with the consequences that come from believing it, while utilitarianism identifies moral *goodness* with consequences that come from an *act*. Utilitarianism says that the only intrinsic good is happiness, and that happiness equals pleasure (whether physical or mental), and that any human act should be judged morally simply by the quality and quantity of its consequences: Does it cause "the greatest happiness (pleasure) for the greatest number"?

Thus, utilitarianism denies the natural law, natural rights, the personalist principle, and the Golden Rule, all four of which are versions of *justice*, in the broad, ancient, Platonic sense of the word. Logically, then, if ninety-nine cannibals would derive greater pleasure from killing and eating one

noncannibal than the pain the one noncannibal would experience by being killed and eaten, that act would be morally
justified logically by the utilitarian principle. Fortunately,
utilitarians are not always logical.

Caiaphas the high priest who authorized Jesus' Crucifixion
was a utilitarian when he reasoned that if we practice justice
and let this innocent rabble-rouser live, rather than practicing
injustice by crucifying him, there will very probably be a riot
and the Romans will come and restore order by murdering
thousands of innocent people. So it is better for one innocent
man to die for the good of his nation than that justice be done.
Justice is not an absolute for utilitarians; only happiness is.

Another obvious problem with utilitarianism, besides denying (1) basic moral principles like the Golden Rule, the personalist principle, and the natural law, and (2) denying justice,
is (3) making moral choices dependent on our *uncertain* and
imperfect knowledge of the *future* and the consequences of our
acts rather than on our *certain* knowledge of the unchanging
moral law and the nature of our moral acts in the *present*. In
other words, utilitarianism "plays God" in assuming that we
have a secure knowledge of the future consequences of actions.
Experience, of course, refutes this assumption.

There is a partial truth to utilitarianism: that ends and purposes and consequences do count. Morality is not merely blind
obedience to a set of rules, and one of the three factors that
influences the moral goodness or badness of any human act
is the surrounding situation or circumstances, which include
the likely future consequences. (The other two are the subjective motive and the objective nature of the act itself, as will
be explained in the next chapter.) A morally good end does
indeed justify a morally good means—that's what a "means"
means. But even a morally good end (like feeding the starv-
ing poor) does not justify a morally evil means (like killing
the rich).

Utilitarianism almost always goes together with moral subjectivism and relativism, and is directly contradicted by traditional natural law morality, in which acts are judged by their own intrinsic nature and by their conformity with universal moral laws.

59

What Makes a Human Act
Morally Good or Evil?

There are at least four different answers to the question regarding what makes a human act morally good or evil.

The first is simply the actor's motive: if your intention is good, that's all that matters. This is moral subjectivism. No one wants his surgeon, financial adviser, or pilot to practice that moral philosophy.

The second is simply the situation. This is moral relativism, since situations are relative, not absolute, and it is also moral skepticism since situations are unpredictable and constantly changing.

The third is simply the nature of the act itself as specified by the moral law as known by one's reason. If this is the only factor, it is legalism and rationalism.

The fourth, which is the answer that is both traditional and commonsensical, is that all three of these factors count, and therefore all three of the first answers are wrong because they are all oversimplifications.

The analogy with the arts is illuminating here. A work of art, such as a novel, has many dimensions: a plot, characters, setting, theme, and style. If any one of these dimensions is defective, it is not a good novel. So with morality: it must be right in all three of its dimensions—the objective and absolute dimension of the nature of the act itself, the subjective and absolute dimension of the motive, and the objective and relative dimension of the situation or circumstances. (There are no absolutely right or wrong circumstances, but there are absolutely right or wrong motives—for example, love or hate, justice or injustice, kindness or cruelty.) We must (1) do the right thing, (2) for the right reason (motive), and (3) in the right way (circumstances).

A good motive does not excuse a bad deed, and a good deed does not excuse a bad motive. And we could even have a good deed *and* a good motive but in the wrong circumstances— such as singing and dancing to make others happy during a military battle, or making love to your spouse when it's medically dangerous.

Another analogy for morality is the organs in the body. If any one of the major organs or systems fails, the whole body fails. All of the organs need to function and cooperate because they are organically interconnected: the goodness of the whole depends on the goodness of all the parts and each part is good by its relation to the whole.

Incidentally, that is why both art and medicine are not only good analogies for understanding morality in theory but also good training in living it in practice. This is also true of farming, which deals with naturally growing organisms. Order in nature and art conditions us for order in morality.

60

Does Virtue Make You Happy?

We often subconsciously think that virtue does not make us happy. Perhaps part of the reason is the subconscious word association between *duty* and toilet training, between *duty* and *doo-doo*.

But in fact and in long-range experience, both in individual lives and in the life of the human race, it is the opposite: moral character and behavior in fact makes us happier, and immorality always makes us unhappy deep down and in the long run, even though on the surface and immediately it strongly appeals to our desire for happiness and can give us a short-lived satisfaction or thrill.

That point—that moral virtue makes you happy and moral vices make you miserable—is the main point of the most famous book of philosophy ever written, Plato's *Republic*. It is the simple lesson we were taught as children, but sometimes the simplest and most fundamental lessons are the ones we forget the most, especially when they are so simple that they do not appeal to our desire to be sophisticated and adult. (But in our culture *adult* is a euphemism for *adulterous*. That's not a joke. Notice which clubs, movies, books, and bookstores are called *adult*.)

The close causal relationship between moral virtue and personal happiness is the reason why both ethical philosophies that focus only on personal happiness, like hedonism and utilitarianism, and ethical philosophies that focus only on moral duty and obedience, like Stoicism and Kantianism, are incomplete and ineffective.

The two Greek words usually translated "happiness"—*eudaimonia* and *makarios*—both have *two* dimensions in their meaning: (1) subjective personal happiness or contentment or satisfaction and also (2) objective rightness or justice or truth. Joy and justice, delight and duty, happiness and holiness are a package deal. They always go together deep down and in the long run, as do misery and mischief, suffering and sin, unhappiness and unrighteousness.

This is true in all areas of life. The happiness of practicing any art or science successfully and well comes only from obeying its laws and requirements through patience and self-discipline. Our passions are like animals: beautiful and with great potential but in need of taming and training. Dogs and cats that share in the life of a human family through loving training are happier than dogs and cats in the wild.

The same is true of our bodies in relation to our souls and, within our souls, of our passions in relation to our reason. The higher perfects the lower rather than suppressing it or rivaling it; as the creator perfects his creation, God perfects man, and grace perfects nature.

61

What Is Conscience?

Just as we often reduce happiness, intuition, and love to feelings, we often reduce conscience to a feeling. But happiness is not just a subjective feeling, for a successful but evil tyrant feels happy when he is torturing his victims, but he is not truly happy.

And intuition is not just a feeling but a seeing, an understanding, when we "see" that justice is a virtue or that triangles must have three sides. And love is not a feeling, for it is commanded of us, and feelings cannot be commanded. So with conscience: it is a seeing of good and evil, not just a feeling. We can "feel good" about an evil act, especially before we do it and are tempted to do it; but that feeling is wrong, not just morally but also mentally. Feelings can be right or wrong—sorrow or joy at another's sufferings, or feeling a love for ugliness or a love for beauty. There are powerful art establishments that are positively allergic to beauty in our culture. If you doubt that, spend a day in New York's Museum of Modern Art. But please be sure you possess no lethal weapons before you go.

If conscience is essentially a seeing rather than a feeling, what does conscience see? Three things: first, the meaning of the whole moral dimension, the moral meaning of good and evil; and second, that moral goodness is obligatory, morally necessary, though not psychologically necessary (that is why we have free will or free choice); and third, which acts, in general, are morally good and which are evil—in other words, some version of the Ten Commandments.

Then, with this as a foundation, our mind understands the nature of the human act, the motivation, and the circumstances, and makes a judgment about whether the concrete particular act is good or evil. This is done by prudence, or practical wisdom.

When we understand that we are morally obligated to do a good act, our selfish passions often pull us in the opposite direction, and when they do, our will must choose to follow either our moral reason and conscience or our passions. Passions can sometimes align with reason, but if they always did, if sin never felt like fun, we would all be saints.

And after we choose evil, and sometimes even *during* the choosing, we feel guilt, experience unhappiness, and either repent and repair the damage or rationalize and justify the evil and thus make it easier to repeat it—which is how we develop vices or bad habits and bad character. We harm ourselves whenever we harm others. And after we choose good, and sometimes also during the choosing, we feel right (because we *are* right; we feel rightly and truly), and this is how we develop virtues or good habits and good character.

Those are the stages of the moral drama: (1) First, conscience (a) issues us into the moral arena, (b) commands us to play for the good side, and (c) shows us the two sides in the battle. (2) Then our practical reason judges how to make the move to rightly play the game. (3) We confront the tempting forces of the enemy and either conquer and tame them or succumb to them. (4) Moral conquest rewards us with happiness, and moral defeat punishes us with unhappiness and guilt, (5) thereby motivating us (in both ways) for the next battle.

If conscience is reduced to feeling, the foundation of the whole moral enterprise (or "game") is undermined. And what is true for individuals is also true for society, for society is only

made of, by, and for individuals, as government is "of the
people, by the people, and for the people." Feelings are easily
manipulated by demagogues. Hitler was elected in 1933 in a
free, democratic election.

62

Aren't There Exceptions to Every Moral Rule?

It may seem that there are exceptions to every moral rule. For instance, the first commandment obligates us all to worship God, but honest and sincere atheism or agnosticism, though mistaken, could be due to invincible ignorance, and to profess a faith you do not have would be hypocrisy, which is worse than honest unbelief. Respect to parents is commanded, but Jesus himself commands us to turn our backs on our families in order to be his disciples if necessary in some circumstances (Lk 14:26). "Thou shalt not kill," but self-defense and just war are examples of deliberate killing that can be right. "Thou shalt not steal," but it is right to forcibly take a weapon from an unjust aggressor. We should not lie, but the Dutch were duty bound to lie to the Nazis when they promised to hide the Jews.

Yet there are no exceptions to the rules or commandments. They are absolute and exceptionless not only because of their origin (divine authority) but also because of their content. They are about the essential and unchangeable nature of the act. But sometimes what appears to be a morally right violation of one of the commandments really is not, since appearance and reality do not coincide, at least to the nonomniscient human mind.

For instance, not all deception is lying, which is a sin against truth—such as in the case of the Dutch hiding Jews from the Nazis. One could say that the Nazis gave up their right to know the truth by their lethal intentions. Or one could say that not all deception is lying, and is often necessary not only for social interactions ("The boss is not in today") but sometimes even to save lives.

With regard to killing, one could also say that self-defense is justified if necessary because the intended murderer has given up his right to life. Or, more simply, one could note that the commandment does not forbid killing as such but only murder. The same God who issued that commandment also authorized capital punishment in ancient Israel.

One could say that forcibly taking a murderer's weapon is not stealing because he has given up his right to that property, or one could say that not all forcible taking of private property is stealing, just as not all forcible killing is murder. The commandments do not forbid all violence. Jesus himself used violence when he whipped the money changers out of his Father's house.

By the way, no *emotion* is always and intrinsically evil, though some (like anger, fear, or sexual desire) are more often to be resisted than followed, and others (like family loyalty) are more often to be followed than resisted. In the case of parents who will do anything to keep their children out of war, even a just and necessary one, this usually good emotion of family loyalty is to be resisted. And it is often good to strengthen rather than weaken sexual passion for the sake of marital intimacy and the pleasure of one's spouse. Anger, which is usually bad, is sometimes very good and right. If one never gets angry, even at radical injustice and harm to innocent persons, one is seriously lacking in a complete moral character. Even hate has its proper object, which is never persons, even evil persons, but things that harm persons, whether the harms are physical (e.g., cancers) or psychological (e.g., drug addiction) or spiritual (sins). The surgeon should have no mercy or pity on his patient's cancer if he really loves his patient, and the same is true of ourselves when dealing with spiritual cancers, whether our own or others'. But the hate of the evil should be motivated only by the love of the good.

For most people, lust is the most passionately strong, the most pleasant, and the most difficult to control of all the emotions. But not all sexual desire is lust. Sexual desire was invented by God, and its purposes are very good: (1) intimacy and union, (2) expression of personal love, and (3) procreation, which is the most literally creative thing we can do because it procreates the only things in the universe that have nonrelative, noncalculable, and nonnegotiable value. Saint Thomas says that sexual pleasure must have been greater, not less, before the Fall, because everything in human nature is more joyful and alive in its perfect natural state than in its fallen and twisted state. Lust does not mean sexual passion as such, or too much passion, but disordered passion—disordered either because it is directed to the wrong persons or because it is selfish, for one's own pleasure rather than another's.

If God is the only absolutely absolute absolute, then whoever and whatever commands us to disobey him or leads us away from him must be disobeyed even if they are lesser authorities such as parents or the state. As the disciples said when they were accused by those who had both religious and political authority in Israel, "We must obey God rather than men" (Acts 5:29). It would be not only unfaithful but also unreasonable not to have absolute fidelity to the God who is the Absolute Good. The principle that justifies apparently "fanatical" obedience to God is simply the three-Rs principle of a right response to reality; and this principle is known by reason, not by faith.

Part VII

Social and Political Ethics

Is the State Natural or Artificial (a "Social Contract")?

Plato, Aristotle, and nearly all classical premodern philosophers held that the state, or civil society, as well as families, tribes, and races, was natural or inherent in the teleology of human nature. This was based on an acceptance (1) of universals like human nature (2) and of objective, universal teleology—two ideas that became unfashionable in modern philosophy with its tendency toward nominalism about universals and its subjectivism about purposes, goals, aims, or ends.

In modern times, we find both optimists about man like Rousseau and pessimists about man like Machiavelli and Hobbes teaching that man by nature, or in "the state of nature," was apolitical; and that civil society as such—and not just particular forms of it like monarchy, aristocracy, or democracy—was invented by a "social contract" rather than being inherent in human nature. This is the position of most (but not all) influential modern philosophers, such as Machiavelli, Hobbes, Locke, Rousseau, and Marx. They see the whole political dimension as invented and posited by man's will rather than preexisting and discovered as part of the inherent teleology of human nature.

Positivism means the philosophy that holds that ethics is "posited" or chosen by man's will, like the rules of a game, rather than discovered by the mind, like the laws of natural science. There is a natural connection between ethical positivism and political positivism, the philosophy that holds that the very existence of the state, not just the laws it enacts, is a human invention and neither divine nor natural, as the family is natural. The connection between ethical positivism and political positivism is not a necessary one, since only some political positivists are also positivists concerning ethics in general, like Hume and Mill and Nietzsche, but others are not.

The ancients did not deny that different forms of the state, with different rules, were invented by different peoples at different times. But they added that there was also observable in human nature a universal and unchanging political telos, a natural impetus toward a public, civil domain that would include many individuals, families, tribes, and races; and that this was as much an inherent dimension of human nature as language, humor, games, dancing, and sex (to take five different examples). None of these were invented at a certain time in history by the will of certain individuals. They are universal, wherever mankind is found, although the forms they take in different times, places, and cultures are particular, changing, and chosen.

In fact, it is only because these dimensions are inherent, natural, and universal in man that there can be different invented versions of them. In politics this is the will of the people—the social contract—when it is free, and the will of the ruler(s) when it is not. In language, it is the development of different languages among different peoples. In humor, it is different kinds of *things* that different cultures find humorous, and different ways of *expressing* that humor. In sex, it is different preferences and customs as well as different social norms of behavior. In the arts, it is the different forms, customs, and preferences in poetry, music, architecture, and dancing— arts that are found in all cultures. In morality, it is the different moral *emphases* and different *applications* of universal moral principles, but always against the background of the basic principles and a universally felt demand to obey them, as well as a very strong consensus about what particular actions constitute good and evil behavior in the areas of human life that are universal, such as religion, family, sex, language, property, and work. Exceptions are very few and confined (e.g., the meaning of theft among the Roma), except for the modern "sexual revolution."

Because positivism is the typically modern position, it is often labeled "progressive." This is an example of the fallacy of equivocation, which here confuses factual judgments with value judgments. The factual judgment, which is true, is that philosophers in our culture did tend to change from political naturalism to political positivism, that is, from believing that politics is natural to believing that politics is artificial, so that positivism is the *newer* position. But the *value* judgment that positivism is not just newer but also *truer*, or *better*, than political naturalism is not logically contained in or entailed by the *factual* judgment that it is newer, unless one assumes the premise that everything newer is better—which is absurd, and which would entail the conclusion that Nazism was better than the democracy it replaced simply because it was newer. In one sense Nazism was progressive, in another sense it was regressive. The same could be said about the sexual revolution today, which has done to many marriages and families and fetuses what Nazism did to Jews.

The point is that progress is not the same as change; progress, properly speaking, means change for the better. When we speak of physical, cultural, or spiritual diseases "progressing" we speak equivocally. The same is true of the terms *conservative* or *traditional*. Whether that is good or bad depends on the nature of the things that are being conserved or handed down. The value judgment depends on the what, not on the when. "Conserving" the planet's ecological environment can be a "progressive" cause; and either lies or truths can be handed down as part of "tradition." Ambrose Bierce, in his cynical book *The Devil's Dictionary*, defined *conservatives* as "those who are enamored of existing evils" and *progressives* or *liberals* as "those who wish to replace them with new ones." There are only two fields in which the newer is always or almost always the better: science and technology. It is not true of art, philosophy, morality, or religion. There is no automatic progress in beauty, truth, or goodness; in happiness or holiness; in sanity or sanctity.

The main reason for thinking that political positivism is better is that it seems to increase the scope of human freedom and choice. If we invented the state, as we invented a game, we can do with it whatever we choose. If not, not. The main reason for thinking that political positivism is worse is that man is fallen and foolish, while only God is totally trustable, so increasing the scope of man's mind and will and decreasing that of God and of the human nature he designed may be regressive instead of progressive.

This naturally leads to the question, Isn't freedom an intrinsic good, and isn't that the reason why democracy, which maximizes freedom, is the best form of government? These are two of the questions we shall take up in later chapters (67 and 68).

64

What Is the Ideal State?

One possible answer regarding what the ideal state is, is that this is the wrong question because there is no kind of state that is ideal for all times, places, and cultures. To a certain extent this is obviously true (e.g., democracy seems better than monarchy for intelligent and moral people but not for barbarians), and it is equally obvious that moral virtues like honesty, justice, kindness, friendship, cooperation, and self-sacrifice are needed if *any* form of political association is to work. The question is whether there is one that works best, and if so, which is it?

Plato believed that it was an aristocracy—that is, a state ruled by aristocrats. But we moderns instinctively misunderstand that, in three ways. First, *aristocrats* literally means not the richest or the most powerful but the *best* people. In that sense it is almost by definition the best government. Second, Plato thought the best people were the *wisest* people, not the richest or most powerful. Third, he thought that the wisest people were those who, like Socrates, did not arrogantly claim to be wise, like the Sophists, but to be humble *lovers* of wisdom, which is what the word *philosophers* literally means. The rulers he recommended were not absent-minded philosophy professors in ivory towers but people like Socrates.

But Socrates deliberately avoided politics—even though politics in ancient Athens, very unlike politics in current America, was considered a high and honorable thing. For his "divine voice" that guided him throughout his life commanded him to avoid it. Socrates, in contrast to Plato, said almost nothing about politics. The same is true of Jesus, in contrast to Muhammad.

Aristotle, in disagreement with Plato, believed that no one of the three possible answers to the question of who should rule was intrinsically the best one; neither one, a few, or many; neither monarchy, aristocracy, or democracy. The three things that determined good or bad politics for Aristotle were (1) a rule of law rather than of will, (2) the happiness of the citizens (*happiness* meaning both subjective contentment and objective virtue or goodness), and (3) the friendship of the citizens, which he ranked even above justice in importance.

Aquinas opined that the mixed regime was best, with elements of monarchy, aristocracy, and democracy—that is, with order centralized in a monarch, decisions made by the best and wisest, and all citizens involved in and responsible for their governing. America is based on a form of that mix, with the separation of the three branches or powers of government: the executive (the semimonarchical president), the judiciary (the aristocrats or "experts" on justice, the courts), and the legislative (congress, elected by and responsible to all citizens); and also, within the legislature, both a small, "elitist" body (the Senate) and a larger, more egalitarian one (the House of Representatives), each part balancing and correcting the others.

Ancient political philosophers almost always saw the ultimate purpose of the state as to help people to their telos or natural end. Modern philosophers, who tend to nominalism, more typically deny both a universal (and universally known) human nature and a universal (and universally known) natural moral law; and they tend to reduce happiness to subjective contentment, and therefore reduce the purpose of the state to utilitarian things like an efficient economy and military protection rather than moral improvement. The problem with ignoring the moral dimension in politics is that it allows cads, liars, narcissists, and even tyrants to be embraced and elected because they promise the people the modern version of the Roman "bread and circuses."

Dorothy Day, who was something like the American Mother Teresa, quoting Peter Maurin, defined "a good state" very simply as "a state that made it easy to be good." Most of the ancients would agree with that definition, but most moderns would not, because the consensus has broken down about what goodness is, what happiness is, and whether goodness, rather than money, sex, and power, is the way to happiness.

C. S. Lewis, in line with Dorothy Day, says: "The State exists simply to promote and to protect the ordinary happiness of human beings in this life. A husband and wife chatting over a fire, a couple of friends having a game of darts in a pub, a man reading a book in his own room or digging in his own garden—that is what the State is there for. And unless they are helping to increase and prolong and protect such moments, all the laws, parliaments, armies, courts, police, economics, etc., are simply a waste of time."[1] The state, like the Sabbath, was made for man, not man for the state.

But that means we must know what man is and what the good for man is if we are to have a state that fosters it. We cannot avoid having a philosophy behind our politics. Which brings up our next question.

---

1   C. S. Lewis Institute, "God's Purpose for the Believer, the Church, and the Creation," May 2011, https://www.cslewisinstitute.org/wp-content/uploads/2021/05/Reflections_2011_05-Gods -Purpose-for-the-Believer-the-Church-Creati-232.pdf.

65

Should the State Have an Official, Public Philosophy of Man and Human Life?

Once again, ancients and moderns disagree regarding if the state should have an official, public philosophy of man and human life. The ancients would argue, with Cicero, that you cannot avoid philosophy, for if you try to do that, that becomes your philosophy. It is a stupid philosophy, but it is a philosophy.

On the other hand, modernity is increasingly suspicious of metanarratives about the meaning of human life, happiness, and morality. This is typified by Justice Anthony Kennedy's famous "mystery" passage in *Planned Parenthood v. Casey,* which based the defense of the right to choose to murder your own unborn children on the premise that "at the heart of liberty is the right to define one's own concept of existence, of meaning, of the universe, and of the mystery of human life."

This opinion is not a repudiation of a political philosophy in the name of liberty; it is a political philosophy that defines liberty. It is the philosophy of nihilism, skepticism, subjectivism, and relativism. It is nihilism because it denies the existence of a real meaning and purpose and end that we can discover rather than create. It is skepticism because it claims to know that we cannot know the objective truth about these things. It is subjectivism because it reduces objective and universal truth about these things to each individual's "own" personal opinions. It is relativism because it makes the whole meaning of life, of existence, of the universe, and of meaning relative to the individual's will to create his "own" conceptions of them. It is, finally, the clinical definition of insanity: the inability or refusal to distinguish one's own personal, subjective thoughts, feelings, and desires from the real world.

It is also unlivable. If a state actually believed and practiced this philosophy, it would not have any principles for fighting a just war, abolishing slavery, investing in education, or trying cases in court by a standard of justice. Why spend billions of dollars educating people without knowing what people are, what value they have, or what they are for? You can't make political decisions without premises that are philosophical: anthropological (what people are), ethical (what value people have), and teleological (what people are *for*).

If the state is a natural outgrowth of smaller public communities such as villages, clans, and families—and if families are made of, by, and for individuals—then the state can no more live sanely without answering these questions than an individual can.

The fact that people disagree about the answers to these great questions is no obstacle to having a public philosophy. Every state, like every city and every family, must live and work by certain rules, and rules cannot be arbitrary and random, like a roulette wheel, but must be based on reason, which is a claim to know something about the nature of objective reality.

Science is a word that derives from *scio*, the Latin word for "know." Dreaming, feeling, desiring, and willing are not *knowing*. To know, as distinct from to dream, to feel, to desire, or to will, has as its object *truth*, and truth means conformity to *reality*. This most fundamental meaning of science applies to philosophical and political science as well as to sciences like physics, math, and biology, differing only in the narrowness or broadness of the subject matter and the method. How ironic that a culture that values science, practices science, and succeeds in science more than any other culture in history has ever done should take such a radically unscientific attitude toward the most important questions of all.

There is also a logical self-contradiction in the notion of the good state being the state that does not confess or profess or teach or require any answer to the important philosophical questions, for one of those questions is what a good state is. How can a good state be one that does not know what a good state is? That is logically self-contradictory and practically self-destructive.

66

Should Church and State Be Separated?

(*Church* in the phrase "church and state" is taken broadly to mean whatever institution has religious authority. So the issue is about the public and institutional relationship between religious and political authorities.)

In our time and place, people are rapidly becoming less religious and more political; less passionate and committed to religion and more to politics. They are increasingly "religious" about their politics—that is, more passionate about it and more willing to prioritize it—and more "political" about their religion—that is, willing to judge it by political standards, reduce it to their version of social justice, and make it instrumental to their politics. That is simply a sociological fact about our time.

This "religionizing of politics" should not be surprising to religious believers, for if God created and designed us to need him, then when we abandon the true God, it is inevitable that we will erect some idol, some substitute god, to put first. And politics is probably the most popular candidate. *Something* has to be first. If it's not the true God, it's got to be some false god.

Probably the only other candidate that can generate such "religious" passion is sex. It's a cliché that you should not discuss religion, sex, or politics because those are the issues that generate the most heat, the most controversy, the most passion: God, Caesar, and Aphrodite. All three are running for office, for the position of president of your soul.

Jesus told us to "render therefore to Caesar the things that are Caesar's, and to God the things that are God's" (Mt 22:21). That assumes (1) that God is God, (2) that Caesar is Caesar, and (3) that Caesar is not God. In that sense, it assumes a basic separation of powers and authorities. Jesus did not run for president. In fact, he ran in the other direction, literally: he ran away when his followers wanted to make him king (Jn 6:15). Jesus was crucified not first of all by Roman soldiers but by those who put Caesar first, who shouted, at Jesus' trial, "Crucify him!" for "We have no king but Caesar" (Jn 19:15), and by Pilate, who obeyed them.

But Jesus connected religion and politics in a positive way when he commanded Peter to pay his and Peter's taxes to Caesar, even though Caesar was a pagan, idolatrous tyrant (Mt 17:24–27; 22:17–21).

And Saint Paul commanded the Roman Christians: "Let every person be subject to the governing authorities. For there is no authority except from God, and those that exist have been instituted by God" (Rom 13:1).

So it is clear from the data that (1) there is a proper relationship between religion and politics; (2) that religion is higher; (3) that the two are not identical but separate; (4) that neither one should simply replace the other; (5) and that religion affirms politics even if politics does not affirm religion. All that is pretty vague, and what that should look like in concrete detail has been up for grabs for two thousand years.

In one sense the separation of church and state is not a controversial question at all, because these two institutions are in fact separated and distinct everywhere except in the theocracy of Old Testament Israel. The issue is about the extent and nature of the separation.

In Jesus' time Rome was a nearly totalitarian dictatorship, but it granted religious freedom to all religions as long as, when pressed, they would accept the authority of Caesar over and above any other authority, including their religion. This is why Rome did not persecute any religions except Judaism and Christianity: because Jews and Christians worshipped a God whose authority was greater than Caesar's and which had the right to judge Caesar rather than be judged by him.

Thus, Jesus' famous dictum to "render therefore to Caesar the things that are Caesar's, and to God the things that are God's" was not a simple approval of the existing fact of the separation of church and state, but was politically revolutionary and dangerous to the pagan Roman mind, because what Jesus believed belonged to God was, implicitly, *everything*, since God was the Creator of everything. Authority over a thing belongs to its author, whether that thing is a book or a universe.

But this same God who claimed authority over Caesar *gave* authority to Caesar. That is why Jews and Christians had a religious motive for fidelity and obedience to the state as long as it did not demand infidelity and disobedience to God. The justification for "Let every person be subject to the governing authorities" was that "There is no authority except from God, and those that exist have been instituted by God" (Rom 13:1)—not directly, by divine revelation, as in Old Testament Israel, but indirectly, by divine providence. That is why Saint Paul, like Christ, also explicitly ordered Christians to pay their taxes (vv. 6–7).

Two opposite reasons for favoring a separation of church and state are (1) the antireligious argument that religion is inherently bad, or at least bad for politics, and (2) the religious argument that politics is usually, or always, bad for religion. There is a practical point to the second argument, for politicizing religion has, historically, always corrupted it. Thus, the two extremes of the antireligious and the religious, ironically, may agree on this issue of wanting a separation.

That is nice and clean in theory, but inevitably concrete issues bring religion and the government, whatever it is, into conflict. There may be a separation, but it is not a total divorce; and even if it is, the ex-spouses still have to communicate and cooperate about the children. Arguments between the two sides happened repeatedly even in the Middle Ages, when all the governments in Christendom were explicitly Christian and no one talked about a separation of church and state. It happens also today when almost everyone agrees with the separation of church and state.

The issue that was most cutting for the early Church was war. Many Christian converts (though not all) left the army, either because they believed war in general was wrong or because they believed that the particular wars Rome was fighting were wrong. Pacifism has always been an option, although a minority option, for Christians. (See chapter 72.)

Today the most divisive specific issue that divides Christ from Caesar is government support for abortion, which is seen as murder by Christians and, for that matter, all who believe in the natural moral law known by reason and in the data of modern biological science. It is significant and ironic that the same people who ignore what science tells them about unborn human beings appeal to what science tells them about climate change, vaccination, and evolution; and that those who appeal to what science tells us on those "liberal" issues ignore what it tells us on the "conservative" issue of abortion.

As distinct from the question of philosophical principles, the question of what ought to be the particular forms taken by the legal and institutional separation and distinction of the political and religious authorities, and how these two institutions are to best relate to each other, are far from clear and obvious, remain controversial, and have changed very much both in historical fact and in Christian opinion. The Koran claims to have detailed divine revelation about the ordering of society; the New Testament does not.

67

Is Democracy the Intrinsically Best Form of Government?

Intrinsically means "by its own essential nature" as distinct from "according to changing circumstances." *Democracy* means literally rule (*krasos*) by the *demos*, the people at large.

There are three possibilities regarding if democracy is the intrinsically best form of government: that democracy *is* intrinsically best; that it is *not* intrinsically best because another form of government is intrinsically best; or that democracy is *sometimes* the best, or currently the best, but perhaps not the best for other people in other times, especially for primitive or barbaric or morally undisciplined times or peoples.

Plato thought that democracy was intrinsically flawed for the simple and (to him) obvious reason that the best government means rule by the best people, the people who are the most qualified to rule, which means the wisest rather than all equally; and therefore that means that either aristocracy or monarchy is better than democracy almost by definition.

And if we lovers of democracy were to answer Plato and say that we defend a representative democracy in which the people at large elect those they consider the most fit to govern, in other words, the moral and intellectual aristocrats, Plato would reply that there is no reason for believing that the judgment of the people at large is any more trustable regarding *whom* to trust to govern, and thus whom to elect, than their judgment is trustable regarding *how* to govern.

Most people throughout modern Western civilization believe that democracy is indeed the intrinsically best form of government, either (1) because it gives the most people the most freedom; or (2) because the right to govern ought to be dependent on the consent of the governed, at least if both the governors and the governed are adults; or (3) simply because it has worked out better in practice and made most people happy and satisfied.

The first reason depends on the premise that freedom is an intrinsic good, thus the more of it, the better. This will be discussed in the next chapter.

The second reason seems to confuse and conflate physical adulthood with moral adulthood—an identity refuted simply by noting the meaning of "adult" films, bookstores, and clubs in our society.

The third reason assumes that happy people are good people, and ignores the point that even the utilitarian philosopher John Stuart Mill admitted, that "it is better to be Socrates dissatisfied than a pig satisfied."

My point here is not to defend Plato or to attack democracy, but to open the issue.

Aristotle did not believe that any one form of government—by one, by a few, or by many—was intrinsically and therefore always the best one, but he noted, even in his day, that democracy was becoming increasingly popular and monarchy increasingly unpopular. He also said that democracy was the intrinsically *safest* form of government because it resisted the concentration of power in one or a few, who could do the most damage if they had the most power. This argument implies that the best possible government as well as the worst would be monarchy or aristocracy, as Plato said, for "the corruption of the best is the worst." But Plato also believed that democracy naturally led to tyranny because its excess of freedom broke down law and order, thus paving the way for a tyrant to restore it, as it did, briefly, with Napoleon and Hitler. However, this seems a historically weak argument because tyranny seems even more unstable than democracy. Hitler's "thousand-year Reich" lasted all of twelve years.

There are two arguments for democracy. The bad one is that people are good, and the good one is that people are bad. The bad argument is that everyone is so wise and virtuous that everyone ought to be given as much freedom and power as possible. The good argument is that no one is so wise and virtuous that they ought to be given very much power; the danger should be dissipated, not concentrated.

Notice that *freedom* connotes something that seems to us intrinsically good (see the next chapter), while *power* does not. We readily admit, with Lord Acton, that "power tends to corrupt, and absolute power corrupts absolutely," but we do not say that about freedom. Yet the two are at least similar and overlapping: we are deprived of both by death, disease, imprisonment, torture, capture, chains, paralysis, weakness, and poverty. We at least should be as thoughtful and critical about freedom as we are about power if we want to preserve our political regime that values it so much.

Today, democracy, though increasingly popular, is still in its experimental stage. No one knows whether it will last and succeed. If its success depends on the wisdom and virtue of its citizens, then its future is no more inevitable than the future wisdom and virtue of its citizens is inevitable. The wisest prophets do not predict but only warn. America's prophets, our founding fathers, were clear that giving rule (*krasos*) to the people (*demos*) would work only for a wise and moral *demos*. So its future is up to each one of us.

68

Is Freedom an Intrinsic Good?

The most obvious attraction of democracy is that it increases freedom, both of the people in general over their rulers and of individuals over their own lives. If freedom is an intrinsic good, that seems to close the case in favor of democracy. If not, the issue is still open.

But *freedom* means many different things. Two different kinds of freedom are the free choice of the will, which indeed is intrinsic to human nature and therefore universal, and also an intrinsic good, just as intelligence is; and political freedom, which is not intrinsic since it exists in varying forms and amounts in different societies, and which may or may not be an intrinsic good.

But freedom does not seem to be an intrinsic good because we cannot have too much of any intrinsic good, but we commonsensically recognize that we can have too much freedom, just as we can have too much power or too much wealth. If freedom is a kind of power and if all power tends to corrupt us, since we are not wise and virtuous inherently but only by choice, then too much freedom can also corrupt us.

And perhaps one clue that we are not inherently wise is the fact that we do not apply this well-known wisdom about the danger of freedom and power to ourselves, only to others. We are suspicious of empowering those who have power over us or over our friends, with whom we sympathize; but we do not resist empowering ourselves. We assume our own wisdom but not that of others. Surely this is unwise, un-Socratic, and lacking in realism and humility.

Errors usually come in pairs. Tyranny and anarchy seem to be opposite errors, with tyranny giving us too little freedom and anarchy too much. It is possible that democracy, in fearing tyranny, fails to fear anarchy, especially if anarchy in the soul is the root cause of anarchy in the society.

Traditional common sense says that freedom is to be judged (and therefore limited) by the higher standards of truth and moral goodness because it is relative to truth and goodness. Lies enslave you; the truth sets you free. Hate enslaves you; love makes you free. Freedom is relative to truth and goodness, and must be judged by it: there is true freedom and false freedom, true love and false love. There are no such things as free truth or unfree truth but there are such things as true freedom and false freedom (for instance, the freedom to addict yourself with drugs).

Whether political freedom and political power are good for us or not depends on two factors. One is how mature we are. Children, traitors, and tyrants should not have the freedom to vote, bullies the freedom to terrorize their victims, or drunks the freedom to drive. The other factor is what we are free from. Freedom from an evil tyrant is good, but freedom from wise and necessary laws is not. Freedom from addiction to drugs is good, but freedom to addict oneself to them, or to anything else, is not. Freedom is relative to truth and goodness, not vice versa.

69

Why Are There "Conservatives" and "Liberals"?

The terms *conservative* and *liberal* are ubiquitous but unclear. They change their meaning with place and time. On this side of the Atlantic and in our era, conservatives are those who want less government authority and liberals more, while on the other side of the Atlantic, and especially in the past, it is liberals who want less government authority and conservatives who want more. Today, liberals tend to see human life as valuable on the battlefield and thus tend more to pacifism than to militarism; but they do not see human life as valuable in the womb—which is the world's most dangerous battlefield today—or, if the individual so decrees, in those who desire euthanasia. Conservatives tend to the opposite inconsistency. But surely the value of human life cannot depend on its location and on the borders of a battlefield or of a nation—or of a womb. Pascal satirizes one soldier's rationalization for killing another by saying that the other was born on the wrong side of the river dividing their countries; and that seems similar to drawing the border at the birth canal.

The term *progressive* is clearer than the term *liberal*, since a conservative, by definition, wants to conserve what is established or traditional, while a progressive wants to change it. But what is traditional in one place or time is not always what is traditional in another, so even these definitions of progressive and conservative (as for or against change) are relative and changing on concrete issues; thus, neither philosophy is intrinsically better than the other.

In fact, Jesus embraces both when he says that a wise householder brings out of his storehouse both things old and things new. On the one hand, Jesus, like all the prophets, is habitually calling us back to and judging things by their origin— for example, marriage (Mt 19:3–9); and on the other hand, he says, "Behold, I make all things new" (Rev 21:5). For he knows that God is both the supreme traditionalist, as the first cause and origin and designing mind of all creation, and also the supreme progressive and end and perfection; he is both "the Alpha and the Omega" (22:13).

The three things we all need the most are faith, hope, and charity. Faith is the conservative virtue, like a plant's roots or a boat's anchor. Hope is the progressive virtue, like a plant's growing stem or a boat's sails. Both are needed to produce the plant's flower or fruit, which is love.

From the point of view of Catholic social ethics, neither of the two political parties in America, one of which is called conservative and the other progressive, gets high marks on human life issues. One party wants more social safety nets and welfare, and favors more immigration, globalization, and internationalization, while the other wants more reliance on individual initiative and more restrictive national borders, and favors national over international or global interests. But these issues, unlike human life issues, are matters of prudence, not principle. Both parties seek to improve the lives of the poor, some by raising taxes and others by lowering them. Both seek peace, some by increasing military spending, some by decreasing it.

One issue clearly separating the two parties is taxes— conservatives wanting to lower them and progressives to raise them. Which economy works better and makes most lives better is not clear. Catholic social morality mandates a "preferential love"[1] for the poor, but does not tell us whether or not to believe in "trickle-down economics," which claims that lowering taxes on the rich helps the poor in the long run. The principles are clear; the prudential practical applications of them are not.

But if any political party claims that the lives of an identifiable segment of the human race are not sacred enough or intrinsically valuable enough to be legally protected from deliberate killing—whether those targeted for slaughter are Jews, Blacks, Whites, slaves, the unborn, or the old—it is clearly and obviously incumbent on the conscience of every Catholic, every Christian, every theist, every religious person, and even every individual with reason and conscience, to disassociate from that party, unless the other party violates this rule even more (e.g., by supporting nuclear war).

That moral judgment is not a personal judgment on the personal guilt of those who abort their own children, but a rational judgment on the act itself. Clearly, the legal abortion of hundreds of thousands of our children a year is the primary social justice issue of our time. It is also the primary environmental issue because the human environment is the most important environment. It is also the primary peace and justice issue, for the killing of one's own innocent children is not an example of peace or justice but of war, violence, and injustice. Opposing the killing of killers (by capital punishment) is reasonable, but to join this to *not* opposing the killing of innocents (by abortion) is simply logically inconsistent as well as contrary to Christian charity to all.

---

1   *Catechism of the Catholic Church*, no. 2448.

70

How Do We Reconcile Solidarity and Subsidiarity, the Common Good and the Individual Good?

The relation between the state and the individual is probably the single most basic question of social and political ethics.

Solidarity connotes the primacy of the common good, and the need to prioritize it, work for it, and even sacrifice for it. Subsidiarity is the principle that the larger organization (nation over state, state over city, city over neighborhood, neighborhood over family, family over individual) must empower and serve, not absorb or replace, the work of the smaller.

The three musketeers implicitly assumed both principles in their slogan "All for one and one for all." So did the movies *Star Trek III* and *Star Trek IV*. In the first, Spock sacrifices himself for the rest of the crew of the *Enterprise*, arguing that "the good of the many is greater than the good of the one"; and in the second, Captain Kirk justifies risking the whole crew to save Spock by arguing that "the good of the one is greater than the needs of the many." Although these two principles seem to contradict each other, we intuitively sense that they do not.

On the one hand, the common good is greater than the private good, and individuals are required to not only contribute to it but also to sacrifice for it. Obvious examples are citizens paying taxes and soldiers, police, firefighters, and first responders risking their lives to defend or save others in the community. One could also argue that the end and goal in taking care of your own health (e.g., by getting vaccinated) is part of the individual's responsibility for the common good. Even private property has as part of its purpose or destination the good of the whole community.

On the other hand, the whole purpose of the state and all of its armies and economies and businesses is to serve its individuals and families. States are not immortal or intrinsically valuable; individuals are. States and civilizations and cultures do not have souls; individuals do. (That is why the strongest obstacle to totalitarianism is faith in the immortality of the soul.)

Thus, the two most common and tempting errors in social and political morality are collectivism and individualism. Politically, socialism and libertarianism are soft versions of those two errors, each ignoring or downplaying one half of this paradox. Totalitarianism and anarchy are the two hard versions of the same error.

Jacques Maritain distinguishes between the person and the individual. The individual is the opposite of the collective, as "the one" is the opposite of "the many" or of the group or class; but the person and the community not only are not opposites but imply each other. For the person has essential dimensions that are communal as well as individual, and therefore requires public loyalty and responsibility as well as private friendship and private property. And the community, or "common-unity," is a union of persons, not things, and persons are always individuals, each one distinct or divided from others and undivided in himself.

But the solution is not simply a reconciliation or a compromise or a balance, as on a seesaw, as if these two goods of themselves by nature oppose each other. In fact, whenever they are in their natural and healthy state, they reinforce each other. On the one hand, the stronger and better individuals are, the stronger and better their social associations will be. On the other hand, the strongest and most lasting societies are ones that are composed of the strongest and freest individuals. These societies foster their freedom rather than diminishing it. On the one hand, the strongest and freest individual is one who is freest from selfish passions and is devoted to others, both individually and privately (in friendships and marriage) and also socially and publicly (in civil and political life). On the other hand, the whole purpose of society is the good of its individual persons.

Community and individuality are both goods, and the good does not oppose the good; only the evil opposes the good.

The mutual reinforcement of these two goods presupposes that the ancients were correct when they said that man is by nature social and political; that the state, or civil society, is natural to man, although its different forms are obviously invented as deliberate and conscious social contracts. (See chapter 63.)

The mutual reinforcement of solidarity and subsidiarity is also the social reflection of the well-known paradox that obsession with your own happiness makes you unhappy, while self-forgetfully working for others' happiness makes you happy. Every religion in the world teaches some version of that paradox. The ultimate reason for the unity of these two dimensions is the nature of God, or ultimate reality, as a Trinity in unity. God himself says both "I" and "we."

On the one hand, every "we" presupposes two or more "I's." Stones, planets, and ants cannot say "we" because they cannot say "I." On the other hand, the individual becomes truly himself only by self-forgetful love, because that is the reflection of the eternal nature and life of Ultimate Reality, in whose image we are made.

How to reconcile, or rather how to perfect and do justice to, both solidarity and subsidiarity, both common and individual goods, in concrete practice, is a matter of prudential judgment, and there is no one political system that alone succeeds in equally avoiding anarchical individualism and totalitarian collectivism. But all concrete attempts at that ideal must be judged by the ideal itself, the abstract principle. Philosophy does not do the work of politics but supplies its principles.

71

What Is the Purpose of Punishment?

The issue regarding the purpose of punishment is not which crimes should be punished, or how severe the punishment should be, or whether death by capital punishment is good or bad, either intrinsically or in our present circumstances. The issue is, What is the reason and justification for public punishment, whether by death, imprisonment, fines, exile, social ostracism, or any other unwanted consequences? This is the most important question of penology.

Three answers have been given: justice, deterrence, and rehabilitation. And the traditional view is that all three ought to be present: that punishment is demanded by justice, that it is necessary to deter others from committing similar crimes, and that it is motivated by the correction and rehabilitation of the offender.

The last two of these motives are parts of charity or altruism. Deterrence is the desire to benefit society and rehabilitation is the desire to benefit the offender. But the justification of the first motive is not charity (at least not directly); it is that justice must be done. That is the reason that is controversial.

What C. S. Lewis calls "the humanitarian theory of punishment" (in his essay by that title) assumes that justice amounts to vengeance ("an eye for an eye, a tooth for a tooth") and contradicts Christian charity, and therefore deterrence and rehabilitation are the only morally legitimate motives for punishment. This sounds more humane and loving; but the problem with it, as Lewis points out, is that unless the punishment is just, it cannot be justified at all, even by the other two standards. In other words, justice is a necessary reason even if it is not sufficient, and the other two reasons are not sufficient even if they are necessary.

For instance, Caiaphas the high priest justified crucifying Christ, whom he knew to be innocent, of civil crimes that he knew Christ did not commit, for the sake of deterring the people from an uprising that would provoke a Roman massacre of the Jews and for the sake of deterring Rome from doing so. Was that truly humanitarian? A modern example: most Frenchmen passionately felt that Colonel Dreyfus was guilty, though he was in fact innocent; but his condemnation in court satisfied the masses, who would likely have rioted if he had been acquitted.

Both miscarriages of justice were justified by the need for deterrence. But deterrence without justice is simply unjust. Tyrants keep law and order by terror, which is an effective deterrent, but it is unjust.

Another problem with substituting the "charity" of deterrence for justice is that making deterrence the primary standard of judgment means making the *predicted* deterrence of future evils the primary standard, which means playing God by claiming to know the future. It also implies the utilitarian principle that the end justifies the means, even if the means is unjust.

The same problem occurs in substituting rehabilitation for justice and making it the only or the primary reason for punishment. Suppose there was a notorious psychopath who intended great evils but who was proved to be guilty merely of shoplifting, while a kindly philanthropist killed a man in a drunken stupor that he deeply regretted. Should the judge give the shoplifter a longer sentence than the murderer because he judged that he needed more "rehabilitation"? Should human judges claim to judge human hearts and souls, or deeds?

We instinctively distinguish an *attempted* killing that did not result in death from an involuntary killing that did. Both are penalized, but the intention of justice must come first, though the other two should also be factored in. For the actual involuntary killing did more public harm than the attempted killing, even though the attempted killing did more harm to the perpetrator than the involuntary killing did. Public trials are primarily about the public good and safety, not the good of the private individual soul. It's God's job to know and judge souls and motives; it's the law's job to know and judge public actions. God is charitable, in fact God is charity itself; but justice is as absolute and nonnegotiable as charity. God himself does not compromise justice but reconciles justice with charity and mercy, on the Cross. We could never have figured out how to do that. Our job is much more modest than God's.

Since justice is the essential criterion in judgment, the other two factors can only modify the judgment, not determine it. "Guilty or not guilty" is the first judgment; what the punishment is to consist of is the second. The punishment must first of all fit the crime, not first of all the criminal.

Those who support "the humanitarian theory of punishment" usually are moral positivists who deny reason's power to know universal and absolute moral laws of justice with certainty. That is ironic because they are really not skeptical *enough* in that they claim to know more than God knows in making their theory of penology dependent on their judgment of the state of the soul of the criminal, in terms of his motives and his need for rehabilitation. They are also utilitarians because their standard of judgment is their supposed knowledge of the future consequences.

How ironic that those who are too skeptical to embrace the natural moral law, which we do know, are not skeptical of their judgment of future consequences (deterrence) and states of soul (how much rehabilitation is needed), which we do not know.

72

Is War Ever Just?

Two questions are often confused regarding if war is ever just. One is whether war is in itself ever a good means of settling a dispute; whether the war itself is a good and just thing. The other question is whether a nation ought to decide to declare war, to initiate or enter a war in some situations. In other words, we must distinguish the war itself and the choice to go to war.

Obviously, war itself is a bad thing, even a stupid thing. "We have differences of opinion and opposing desires. How shall we resolve them? Oh, I have a wonderful idea. Let's all dress up in ugly uniforms and get lethal weapons and find a nice place to go out and kill each other, and whichever side kills the most people on the other side will get what it desires."

There have been some philosophers who thought that war itself was a good thing because it made us strong and tough and heroic: Hegel, for instance, and those who believed in "social Darwinism," the rightness of the survival of the fittest. Nietzsche and the Nazis also believed in the badness of compassion, and the weakness of meekness (kindness). But this is a very small and unpopular minority opinion today.

At the opposite extreme are principled pacifists, who argue that the act of waging war is always and intrinsically evil.

The pacifists' theological argument from the Old Testament is that God himself commanded, "Thou shalt not kill." But God himself mandated capital punishment in ancient Israel, and God cannot command anything that is intrinsically evil. The word translated "kill" in the Ten Commandments means murder, or killing an innocent human being, not all killing, and therefore does not necessarily include killing unjust and threatening aggressors.

The pacifists' theological argument from the New Testament is that Jesus did not use violence (but he *did*, at least once, when he cleansed the Temple of the money changers), and that he stopped the most just war in history—the use of violence by Simon Peter's sword to defend the only totally innocent man in history, himself, in the Garden of Gethsemane when he was about to be arrested. He then miraculously healed the war's only casualty, the right ear of Malchus, the high priest's servant (Lk 22:50–51; cf. Mt 26:51; Jn 18:10)—proving, incidentally, that Peter was left-handed. And Jesus not only commanded Peter to "put your sword back" (Mt 26:52; cf. Jn 18:11) but also gave as his reason the principle that "all who take the sword will perish by the sword" (Mt 26:52). One of Christ's Beatitudes is "Blessed are the peacemakers" (Mt 5:9). He never said "Blessed are the warmakers."

But this does not prove pacifism in principle: firstly, because Jesus is a special case, who came to earth precisely in order to suffer injustice, violence, and death to save us; and secondly, because the man whom Jesus called the greatest of all the prophets, John the Baptist (Lk 7:28), did not tell the soldiers to leave the army when they came to him asking, "What shall we do?" (3:14).

The philosophical arguments for pacifism usually depend on one of two premises: either the principle of the absolute sanctity of human life or the practical consequence that war always does more harm than good; that in war even the "winner" is a loser. As to the first premise, when some of us are responsible for the protection of the lives of others, it is a dereliction of duty to allow those others, if innocent, to be killed precisely *because* human life is indeed sacred. As to the second premise, it is not certain that Athenian pacifism in the face of Persian conquest or the West's pacifism in the face of Hitler would have done more good than harm.

The mainline position that avoids both the extreme of absolute pacifism and the glorification of militarism is the so-called "just war theory," which defines under what conditions the choice to wage war is a just and morally right choice. These conditions are usually listed as the following by both Christians and Muslims (to what extent they have been *obeyed* is a very different issue):

1. that the cause for waging war must be just;
2. that proportionately more good than evil is very likely to result from waging the war;
3. that warring is the necessary and only way of attaining the good or avoiding the evil, and all other means of reconciliation and settling the dispute peacefully have been fairly tried and failed;
4. that the war must be a response, defensive rather than aggressive (the Koran states that "Allah hates the aggressor"[1]); and,
5. especially in an age of weapons of mass destruction, that noncombatants should be spared as much as possible.

The just war theory is in spirit closer to pacifism than to militarism because it makes *not* waging war the default position; it assumes that if the waging of any given war does not meet *all* five of these criteria, it is unjust. And this means that the bar for a just war is at least very high, and that the vast majority of all the wars (that is, the choices to go to war) in history do not qualify as just wars.

For instance, the American Civil War probably could have been avoided and emancipation achieved by patient

---

1   Koran 2:190.

negotiation and gradualism rather than killing. However, given the ideology of Nazism and the personality of Hitler, World War II almost certainly qualifies as a just war. Ghandi's pacifism worked in India because the British, unlike the Nazis, had a moral conscience; but the effect of pacifism in Hitler's Germany would have been simply the murder of all pacifists.

However, the terrorist bombing of civilian targets in London and Dresden were pretty clearly wrong. The nuclear bombing of Hiroshima is a more complex issue, since on the one hand, it avoided the likely consequence of probably half a million deaths, which would have resulted from enforcing Japan's surrender with conventional forces (see criterion 2); but on the other hand, all nuclear bombs kill massive amounts of innocent civilians, thus violating criterion 5. And unless we are utilitarians, consequences cannot be our primary consideration.

The issue of war is a good example of the principle that, on the one hand, moral *principles* are or should be quite clear and absolute, but, on the other hand, their prudential *application* to complex situations is often (but not always) quite unclear and relative, and that the simple-minded passion and conviction of rightness that typifies both sides in every war are usually unjustified. There are in this world no examples of literal, physical wars between immaculate saints and demon-possessed maniacs, only between two groups of morally and mentally defective human sinners.

But the mentality of *spiritual* warfare is an essential part of Christianity. We do have real enemies, but they are not "flesh and blood" but "principalities ... powers ... [and] hosts of wickedness in the heavenly places" (Eph 6:12). The essential theme of the plot of every good story, and therefore of life itself, is the war between good and evil. For, as Solzhenitsyn famously wrote in his *Gulag Archipelago*, the dividing line between the enemies in this war runs not between two nations or empires or civilizations but between the two parts of every human heart.

Appendix: Other Philosophical Questions

Philosophy can be applied to many different fields and subjects:

The philosophy of history: What is the meaning and end of history?

The philosophy of beauty or aesthetics: What is beauty, and what is its value?

The philosophy of art: What is art's end and purpose?

The philosophy of science: What are the limits of science?

The philosophy of education: What is the purpose of education?

The philosophy of technology: How has it changed human life for better or for worse?

The philosophy of humor: Why do we laugh?

The philosophy of religion: What is the secular value of religion?

The philosophy of culture: What is a culture, and what is a culture war?

The philosophy of sexuality: What is the meaning and purpose of sexuality?

The philosophy of evil: What is evil, why does it exist, and how can it be defeated?

The philosophy of language: What is the role of language in perfecting our humanity?

The philosophy of mathematics: In what way are numbers real?

The philosophy of logic: Is there one absolute logic, or is it relative?

The philosophy of mysticism: How do we judge the claims of mystical experience?

The philosophy of philosophy: What is "the love of wisdom"?

The philosophy of love: What are the forms of love, and why does it exist?

The philosophy of happiness: What is it, and how can we attain it?

The philosophy of literature: What is literature, and what does it do for us?

We can philosophize about anything and everything. For instance, I wrote a book on the philosophy of surfing, *I Surf, Therefore I Am.*

Concluding Unscientific Postscript

This book was designed for beginners. (So was Saint Thomas Aquinas' *Summa Theologica*, according to his own very brief introduction.) If you want a slightly more systematic, scholarly, and logical treatment of the basic issues of philosophy, you might try my *Summa Philosophica*, which explores the reasons on both sides of 110 controversial issues in philosophy in the format of Aquinas' *Summa Theologica*.

Perhaps this was your first philosophy book. In order to put it in its proper place, I invite you to make a thought experiment with me, in four steps. Each step is more fantastic than the previous one, but worth pursuing as a thought experiment.

First, suppose you make this first (or nearly first) philosophy book not your last one. Suppose you go on to read other, better, and greater philosophy books.

Suppose, second, that you go on to not only *read* but also *write* other books of philosophy, as I have done.

Third, suppose the books you write, unlike mine, are not only good but great. In fact, they become as well known and universally studied as Plato's or Aristotle's. (I warned you that this was only a thought experiment, an exercise in imagination and fantasy.)

Fourth, suppose you become the greatest philosopher in the world. (That's not as hard nowadays as it used to be; the really great philosophers are all dead.)

Now all that would be a very wonderful thing, because philosophy is the love of wisdom, and wisdom is a very wonderful thing, a precious and glorious and magnificently beautiful thing. Solomon said, "Wisdom is the principal thing; therefore get wisdom" (Prov 4:7, KJV).

But if you are a Catholic (or Orthodox) Christian, you already, actually, literally have something that is not only even more precious but *infinitely* more precious than the highest goal of philosophy, that wonderful thing called wisdom. You have, in actual, literal fact, the most incredible, astonishing, beyond-all-hopes-and-dreams gift ever given. You have what Saint Thomas asked God for when God praised Thomas' wisdom in writing the *Summa* and asked him what he would have as his reward. He answered, "Only Yourself, Lord." Every time you receive Holy Communion, you have the total and infinite Wisdom—that is, a divine Person, Jesus Christ—literally, totally, and fully present in you, Body and Blood, Soul and Divinity. You have him in your body and in your soul, and you have him forever.

Philosophy is our love of wisdom, and that is a very great thing. But Wisdom's love of us is an even greater thing. For God to make the universe out of nothing was an amazingly great thing. But for him to do what he is doing in your life, making a saint out of a sinner, is an even greater thing.